# DR. ROBERT DAWSON

# HOW TO BE HAPPY IN SPITE OF YOURSELF

**BALBOA.**
PRESS

A DIVISION OF HAY HOUSE

Balboa Press books may be ordered through booksellers or by contacting:

Balboa Press
A Division of Hay House
1663 Liberty Drive
Bloomington, IN 47403
www.balboapress.com.au
1 (877) 407-4847

Because of the dynamic nature of the Internet, any web addresses or links contained in this book may have changed since publication and may no longer be valid. The views expressed in this work are solely those of the author and do not necessarily reflect the views of the publisher, and the publisher hereby disclaims any responsibility for them.

The author of this book does not dispense medical advice or prescribe the use of any technique as a form of treatment for physical, emotional, or medical problems without the advice of a physician, either directly or indirectly. The intent of the author is only to offer information of a general nature to help you in your quest for emotional and spiritual well-being. In the event you use any of the information in this book for yourself, which is your constitutional right, the author and the publisher assume no responsibility for your actions.

Any people depicted in stock imagery provided by Thinkstock are models, and such images are being used for illustrative purposes only.
Certain stock imagery © Thinkstock.

Print information available on the last page.

ISBN: 978-1-5043-0978-3 (sc)
ISBN: 978-1-5043-0979-0 (e)

Balboa Press rev. date: 08/29/2017

# DEDICATION

This book is dedicated to my partner Stella. Without her love, support and tolerance of my instinctive moods and her experience and intellect to provide me with a sounding board, this book would not have been written.

# ACKNOWLEDGEMENTS

The writing of this book has been going on in my head over at least four decades. During that time I have been influenced by more academics and students than I could possibly mention.

Dr Albert Ellis and Dr Ian Campbell were most influential on my training as a cognitive behaviour therapist. My undergraduate marks were good but not quite good enough to get into the first graduate training program in Cognitive Behavior Therapy at the prestigious University of Melbourne. On reflection it probably would not have occurred if Dr. Campbell had not seen 'something' in me at my admission interview.

Some twenty years later, the work of neurophysiologists Giacomo Rizzolatti, Giuseppe Di Pellegrino, Luciano Fadiga, Leonardo Fogassi, and Vittorio Gallese at the University of Parma in the 1980s and 1990s on mirror neurons got me thinking about what Dr. Campbell might have seen. Mirror neurons are a neurophysiological explanation for the existence of empathy.

Deep empathy has been described as the ability not just to imagine but to actually *feel* what other people are experiencing. It's the ability to actually enter the "mind space" of another person so that you can sense their feelings and emotions. In a sense, your identity merges with theirs. The separateness between you and them fades away. Your "self-boundary" melts away, so that in a sense – or to an extent – you become them.

Empathy is touted as an important requirement for a therapist, an important strength to understand and help others. But it is also a significant burden if empathy prevents a separation from the distress of others, from establishing clear boundaries between oneself and others. Burn-out is an ever present issue for therapists.

To the extent that density of mirror neurons are inherited I have to acknowledge my genetic inheritance and the influence that my father had on me in championing the rights of trade workers in Australia to get a basic wage. I see my choice to study psychology and work as a therapist as an evolution of this desire to help others and myself.

In my first years of practice, my effectiveness as a therapist was shaped by Brad Levingston. He was my boss and supervised my work in my first professional appointment. Over the next forty years I recharged my enthusiasm for my work by going off on related tangents including taking on teaching roles in Graduate University programs. Being challenged to not only do the "talk" but also demonstrate the "walk" by hundreds of graduate therapy students kept me on my toes and I thank them all.

I still remember the occasion twenty years ago when I was lecturing about paranoia and gave a scenario of a driver noticing that a car had been following closely for the past twenty or so minutes. I asked the group what they thought the driver might have been thinking. One student instantly said that the driver thought "The towing is going well!".

The most recent and profound influence on this book is the work in Evolutionary Psychology and I would like to acknowledge the host of researches in this area.

In my personal, and social life I would like to acknowledge Ken Marshall, Peter Craft, Gary Troedson and John Holmes for the experience of building trust, sharing the pain of competition and keeping me alive in my tumultuous teenage years. To Richard Nelson-Jones, an author and psychology lecturer who told me that the only difference between people that write books and people that don't write books is that "… the people who write books, write books." To Phil Jenkins for inadvertently spurring me to get started. To past relationships for giving me an opportunity to learn more about myself and for shaping the structure of this book. To my children for tolerating my obsessiveness. To my cycling group for giving me an effective tap to drain away the frustration of day to day life.

From my professional life I want to acknowledge the hundreds of clients who have provided most of the examples given in the book and who have inspired me to get this written.

# INTRODUCTION

Most of us have been happy, so we know how good it feels. But our experience of this great feeling is that it does not last. We have been led to think that when it doesn't, there must be something wrong— something wrong with our upbringing, our schooling, our relationships, our work, our friends, with our security, our health, our faith, ourselves, with the world. We become unhappy when we are frustrated that our happiness doesn't last.

Feeling and thinking that there is something wrong, we look for solutions. This search for solutions often leads us to decisions and actions that initially seem to make us happy. These choices are aimed at changing, getting rid of, or avoiding old things and acquiring new things (new house, new baby, new relationships, new friends, new job, new clothes, new car, new bike, new diet, new phone—anything new). But any happiness that comes from these decisions inevitably wears off. When it does, we return to being unhappy and often enough regret our actions. It seems that the consequences of many of our deliberate attempts to be happy have a significant later role in the ongoing focus of our unhappiness (e.g., disappointment, stress, and debt).

This book rests on the idea that there is an important reason happiness is only temporary.

Evolutionary psychology views unhappiness and the many negative feelings associated with sadness—discontentment, frustration, anxiety, anger, depression, guilt, resentment, envy—as essential for survival. These negative feelings of dissatisfaction keep us motivated to do better, to look for improvements. They also keep us on edge and ready for action. They keep our guard up. From an instinctive survival perspective, not happy is the default human condition. Although we have been, can be, and will be happy, happiness is not a natural, ordinary state.

This perspective might seem a bit pessimistic and might lead to thoughts like, "Well, what's the point of surviving if you can't be happy?" Yet this perspective is not saying you can't be happy. You can and will be happy. Random life events, including the positive reactions of others toward you, will ensure that you are happy every now and again. What this perspective is saying is that every episode of happiness you experience has to fade to keep you safe. Instinct makes this so. The pendulum swing of our moods between happiness and unhappiness, contentment and discontentment, satisfaction and dissatisfaction is natural, ordinary, and necessary for our species to thrive.

Swinging moods do not automatically mean that something is wrong.

There are two parts to this book. The first six chapters explain why instinct needs us to be unhappy. They also explain how our unconscious survival instinct ensures that any happiness that does come our way never lasts for very long.

The second part of the book demonstrates how a conscious effort on feelings, thoughts, and actions can initiate and extend periods of happiness when they occur and cushion the dampening impact on our mood when they inevitably fade. The chapters in the second part of the book illustrate this process in a range of life scenarios that we will all face eventually. These situations include:

- Relationships, socializing, breaking up.
- Parenting.
- Work and competition.
- Dealing with bureaucracy.
- Retirement, aging, and chronic pain.

Chapter 7 links the understanding of Part One to the practice of Part Two. "Lifting the Fog of Instinct" details the three-step habit we need to develop to moderate the negative effect of the human survival instinct on the quality of our life. When you realize that your instinct is undermining your happiness and see it for what it is—a normal and necessary automatic reaction to life's challenges—you are on the way to being happy in spite of it.

My work as a clinical psychologist has spanned four decades, and I have been thinking about writing this book for at least the last two of these. What held me up was a missing piece of the puzzle of human psychology—the piece that explained why smart people repeatedly do dumb things. How come people don't seem to learn from history? Until I found this piece, I could only observe this behavior in my clients (and myself) and present strategies to minimize the collateral damage. There seemed to be nothing I could do to prevent this behavior from re-occurring, and I was not ready to put pen to paper.

I initially took nine years to prepare myself to be a therapist—a four-year undergraduate honors degree in psychology, a two-year master's degree in clinical psychology, and three years of researching therapeutic strategies for a doctor of philosophy degree to reassure myself that the therapeutic approach I intended to specialize in was the "right" one. I subsequently began, and forty years later retired from, a career in psychology as a cognitive behavioral therapist. Over this time, I saw many clients, worked as a lecturer in undergraduate and graduate psychology programs in three universities, and trained hundreds of mental health professionals in the skills and strategies of cognitive behavioral therapy (CBT).

Roughly ten years ago, I came across the field of evolutionary psychology. I may have touched on this in my undergraduate courses at university, but I don't remember doing so. My two graduate degrees were very focused on therapeutic strategies. Evolutionary psychology did not come up in either of them. When I started reading about the impact of evolution on human psychology and behavior, the light went on for me. This impact was the missing piece. Here was the reason smart people repeatedly do dumb things.

The first impact of this light-bulb moment was on my therapy. I gradually changed the way I delivered CBT and saw improvements in outcomes for my clients. The second impact of this light-bulb moment was on me. I found it easier to live in my skin. I became more satisfied with myself and my circumstances, less dissatisfied with having to deal with day to day challenges and less obligated to be "perfect".

Having found this missing piece, I am ready to share with you what I have learned during my career as a therapist. The title of this book says it all: *How to Be Happy in Spite of Yourself*. If this title resonates with you in any way, you are ready for it.

This book is about how to become aware of your automatic, instinctive reactions; how to release the emotional tension they cause; how to consciously regulate them with deliberate intention; and how to put intentions into action and create opportunities to be happy in spite of yourself.

Dr. Robert Dawson
BA (Honors), MA (Clinical Psych), PhD

# CONTENTS

# CHAPTER 1
# NEGATIVITY BY NECESSITY

In the beginning, almost everything necessary for our survival was scarce. Obtaining food, water, and shelter required most of our time and effort, and we had to compete for it. Our species survived the beginning and is now the dominant life form on earth, even though we aren't the biggest, fastest, most ferocious animal around.

We lack the size, physical strength, sharp teeth, tough skin, and speed of many other animal species. What we lack in these physical attributes, we make up for with a complex brain. Anthropologists call us *Homo sapiens* (Latin for "wise man"). According to the neuroscientists, there are billions of neurons (brain cells) between our ears. We were never the strongest species, but we proved to be the smartest. We use our "big brains" to observe and learn, adapt, plan, strategize, and improvise. Our intelligence allowed us to discover fire, make weapons, traps, and tools, and to develop hunting and other survival strategies.

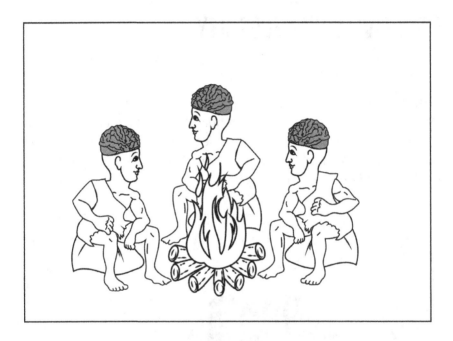

The survival of our species has depended on three fundamentals:

- Fear.
- Speed.
- Safety.

More specifically, we need reaction speed for when things go wrong; the security to minimize the frequency of things going wrong; and fear that safety can't last. Our big brain has allowed us to be the last surviving species of the human genus line. It has taken us out of the Stone Age and is propelling us toward the stars. To achieve this, our brain sacrifices quality of life for the greater goal of life itself, for survival.

While the size of our brain is moving us forward, its complexity has the potential to get us killed along the way. A weakness of our big brain is the potential it has for lots of thinking and for significant delays to occur between the beginning of deliberate thought and the actions that follow. In survival circumstances, conscious thinking slows down reaction time. When faced with situations where the speed of our response is of life-or-death importance, the time it takes to think can get us killed.

In survival situations, we must act, act immediately, and act quickly. No time to think. Just do it!

To handle these emergencies, to save split seconds and hence improve our chances for survival, we have a mechanism of automatic response. This automatic response occurs before conscious thought has even begun. When speed is everything, human actions occur as reflexes to a situation. Our brain has developed the ability to know when there is no time to consciously think about what to do and what might happen when we do, and how that might affect what happens tomorrow. This ability to react quickly without any input from conscious thought is part of our survival instinct.

You glimpse something coming at your face. You don't know what the thing is, you don't know what caused the thing to be heading your way, and you don't know why. You might not even be aware that your hand is up blocking or catching. Analysis and deliberation occur after your reflex action, after you have caught or blocked the missile. There was no time for all that before your hand went up. You first had to survive the object.

Our brain automatically knows when to "reflex." When it does, the action comes before conscious thought—reaction speed is all important. We have a big brain, but in some circumstances, we only use a tiny portion of it to survive.

At a fundamental level, safety for humans is related to the size of the group. We have learned that there is safety in numbers. At an unconscious level, our survival instinct makes us pursue connections with others (including with animals). The more connections we have, the bigger our group. The larger the group, the safer we are.

At a conscious level of thought, the way we feel about connections can be confusing and illogical. For example, "Why should it bother me that just one person doesn't like me?" Rationally it makes no sense that any single person not liking you is a threat to your existence, and therefore you shouldn't care. However, at an instinctive level, being bothered by this makes total sense, because the number in the group of people who like or are neutral toward you has just been reduced by one.

"Be prepared" is a motto for survival. We can't know what the future brings, but we had better have our guard up and be ready. Our survival instinct operates on the principle that "if you snooze, you lose." Instinct does not want you to celebrate your success or feel good about your effort for too long. Enjoyable feelings improve the quality of your life but make you more vulnerable to the possibility of it suddenly ending. From your instinct's perspective, fear is needed to put you on edge and maximize your readiness for survival.

Human instinct compares the current experience with prior experiences that it knows to be threatening and reacts accordingly. The closer the match, the stronger the reaction. There is no off switch. Instinct operates 24/7 outside of our awareness. It can only be affected by how well the brain is functioning. It can't be turned off, but anything that affects the operation of the brain can influence the operation of our instinct—for example, pain, drugs, tiredness, illness.

At birth, we have a small range of survival experience hard-wired into our brain. Initially, only comparisons with this experience—such as hunger, pain, warmth, tiredness, or noise—will trigger survival reactions. Excesses in any of these senses are threatening to our instinct and consequently will trigger a survival reaction: crying.

From birth onwards, the learning that occurs through life experience continuously expands the collection of experiences in the brain that our instinct decides are attractive or threatening. The longer we live, the more adaptive our survival instinct becomes, as the range of experience perceived to be important continuously grows. Life-or-death experiences, as perceived by our instinct, are registered more frequently and in more and more aspects of our day-to-day lives. As we age, our instinctive defensiveness and focus on survival become more dominant as we have more experience with life and learn about more and more things that can hurt us.

In spite of the automatic influence of instinct on our feelings and behavior, we can make satisfaction and happiness last if we take deliberate action. If we don't consciously intervene, the increasing influence of our survival instinct as we age will progressively shorten experienced moments of happiness and satisfaction and lower the quality of our overall life experience.

**Instinct puts survival ahead of satisfaction and happiness.**

Instinct continuously taps into our senses—sight, sound, smell, frustration, tension, pain, and so on. It's like someone listening in to your phone conversation without you being aware of it. It is constantly looking for the signs and sources of danger. It takes over when new sensory information matches stored information that is important for survival.

Survival triggers are of two general types:

1. First, there is sensory information that is hard-wired into the human genetic blueprint (DNA). Examples of these triggers for a newborn baby include loud noise, bright light, heights, hunger, pain, smell.
2. Second, there are triggers that have been learned from the experience of thousands of generations to precede a survival situation. A good example of a survival trigger is attention (being noticed). If others do not notice you, you have no chance of support. The importance of recognition makes information on Facebook a survival trigger.

**Instinct uses physical arousal to motivate behavior.**

When instinct registers a match between a current situation and a stored survival trigger, it dumps natural stimulants into our brain chemistry. These natural stimulants intensify our sensitivity to all our physical sensations, and we consequently take more notice of them.

Regardless of whether these physical sensations are experienced as unpleasant (e.g., fear) or pleasant (e.g., attraction), increasing sensitivity to them progressively prevents us from paying attention to anything else.

The increasing sensitivity caused by our physical arousal grabs our attention, eventually blocks all conscious thought, and forces us into action to seek relief from our heightened arousal.

**In the human species, strong physical arousal (strong emotion) has the power to dominate attention and control human behavior.**

Look around you. Read the media. Watch the news. How often do you see smart and talented people doing dumb and awful things? How often do you see people repeatedly doing this?

Under the influence of intense physical sensations, we can and do treat each other very badly.

Research on brain structure and chemistry indicates that the sensory matching process of instinct occurs in an area of the brain that roughly lies level with the bridge of your nose and in the region right between your ears.

In this region of the brain called the limbic system, the information from our senses comes together before being sent on for analysis in the area of the brain above our eyes—the frontal cortex.

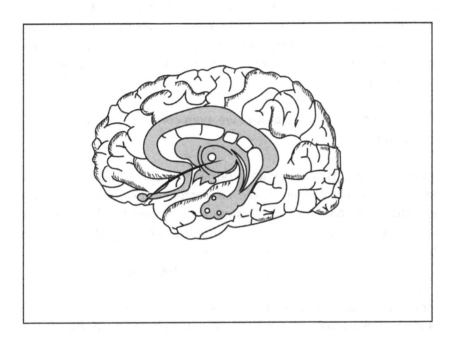

Only when information from our senses reaches and is analyzed in the frontal cortex are we able to understand what is going on. For example, a series of sounds interpreted in the frontal cortex may be recognized as words or a familiar song. A string of marks on a page could be recognized as a bunch of words that make up a sentence.

However, before the sounds or marks arrive in the frontal lobe, instinct has analyzed them in the limbic system and looked for matches with survival triggers. If a match occurs, an instinctive reaction of increased arousal occurs and accompanies the sounds and marks on their journey to the frontal cortex. This additional information means that when we interpret the meaning and make assumptions about what we are experiencing, instinct and heightened arousal prejudice the outcome.

*Dr. Robert Dawson*

## Instinctive reactions bias the analysis of our day-to-day experiences.

When the limbic system decides we are facing a survival situation, it triggers physical arousal. Our freedom of will or freedom of choice that we assume we ultimately have and hold ourselves and others responsible for is biased at best and at worst can be completely suppressed. Before we even realize we have choices, what those choices might be, and what the consequences might be, our limbic system has matched incoming sensations with pre-existing survival triggers, has initiated defensive action, and has generated arousal that biases our understanding and our responses.

## Our reactions are biased before we even consciously know what is happening.

Since it is the intensity of physical arousal that instinct uses to control us, pre-existing levels of arousal make it easier for instinct to affect us in any new situations. That is, existing frustration (high arousal) is likely to cause a person to overreact to a new frustration, even if the frustration about the new situation is minimal. This overreaction is what is happening when we see people responding strongly to trivial situations.

For example, conditions of chronic pain, tiredness, anger, and anxiety cause high frustration. Hence, people suffering these conditions are more likely to overreact suddenly, defensively, and illogically to a new frustrating situation. If we consider this sudden overreaction as an instinctive response to the sum of pre-existing frustration plus current frustration, the apparent overreaction can make sense.

Instinct is continuously scanning for survival triggers. It, therefore, has a mostly negative bias. It is always on the lookout for what is going wrong and what could go wrong. Even in very favorable situations, instinct is constantly monitoring the situation and your performance for anything that could spoil the moment. We have no real day-to-day awareness of our instinct at work other than the fluctuation of our feelings. There is also no way of deliberately shielding ourselves from its influence (other than with mind-altering drugs). Instinct has no on or off switch.

10

Improving the quality of life requires an awareness of the ongoing workings of your survival instinct. It requires deliberate effort to expose it when it is negatively impacting you in situations that are not life-threatening. Once you are aware, you can use and improve strategies to inject more of your conscious mind into your life experience. You can clear away the fog of your instinct.

The evolution and the survival of our species revolves around the experience of safety in numbers. Instinct has learned that if you are not in a group, you are vulnerable, without support. However, the extent of support that you get from any group depends on the power of the group and your relative importance in the group. If you are in a group but the group hardly notices, you don't qualify for much group support. You will be vulnerable when a threat comes around. Your survival instinct operates on the principle that to be safe, you have to be noticed—to have some relative importance and approval. Survival needs recognition in its many different forms, including approval, relative importance, respect, and validation.

Day-to-day changes in your relative importance in the group determine the activity level of your instinct and the extent to which it impacts your feelings and behavior. Yesterday your instinct estimated your recognition in the group to be high, and you felt pretty good. Today your instinct views your recognition in the group as having weakened, and your mood is not as good as yesterday. Tomorrow your instinct anticipates your acceptance in the group slipping even further; you are getting anxious in advance. When instinct wants action from you to satisfy its need for recognition, it agitates you with bad feelings. It does this with *comparisonitis* and *catastrophizing*.

## Summary.

- **Instinct is concerned with survival, not with quality of life.**
- **Instinct uses emotions to influence our thoughts and behavior.**
- **Most of the time we are being influenced by our instinct without realizing it.**
- **If you don't notice and intervene in this influence, then whatever you are, have, or have accomplished will never be good enough.**
- **We can consciously intervene and dampen the impact of instinct on our happiness.**
- **Understanding the importance instinct gives to recognition, approval, and relative importance provides us with the tools to be happy more of the time.**

# CHAPTER 2
# COMPARISONITIS

Comparisonitis is the compulsion to compare oneself to others to determine one's relative importance. From your instinct's perspective, being unimportant in a group or on the edge of a group is the equivalent of being in a life-threatening situation. Your vulnerability to threat increases as your relative importance in the group changes in any negative way. Instinct is continually making these comparisons without us being aware; comparisonitis is unconscious.

When the result of comparisonitis points to diminishing relative importance, instinct uses catastrophizing to create emotional agitation. Catastrophizing likewise occurs at an unconscious level but can also happen at a conscious level. Catastrophizing inserts uninvited thoughts into our consciousness and makes mountains out of molehills. Catastrophizing magnifies a situation into being far worse than it is. It stresses how awful, terrible, and unbearable the situation is. Catastrophizing occurs about the past, the present, and the future.

In a life-and-death situation, you have to be seen to be helped. Not being noticed or supported can be lethal. If instinct rates your situation as life-and-death, it prioritizes speed over logic. It dumps adrenalin into the blood stream to accelerate reaction speed and muscle power enabling extreme behavior aimed at getting attention, approval, or increasing relative importance. In the heat of the moment, instinct doesn't care about collateral or subsequent damage. Survival is its only priority, and there is no concern for analyzing the possible consequences of what is done to get attention, approval, or relative importance.

If the situation is not life-and-death, a drop in relative importance is not lethal. In such a situation, the unconscious process of using strong physiological reactions to prioritize speed over common sense is unnecessary, excessive, and fatiguing. Repetitive comparisons wear you out mentally, and catastrophizing wears you out emotionally. Together, they undermine your energy to perform and achieve.

Comparisonitis evaluates the present with the past and an anticipated future. Even in a favorable present environment, comparisonitis readily finds negative comparisons with the past and future. Unwanted comparisons mean that any satisfaction and security experienced in the present will not last for very long. A forward-looking comparison might anticipate that your current group standing could be threatened in the future by envious others. They may unconsciously decide that your success has lessened their value in the group, and they will be out to devalue your approval rating to improve theirs. You have seen or personally experienced this happening. It's a tendency to discredit or disparage those who have achieved notable wealth or prominence in public life. People can react negatively to the success of others and look for ways to diminish it. From hero to zero in no time at all—that is your instinct's fear. On the other hand, a backwards-looking comparison might assess your current satisfaction to be less than you felt last time from the same achievement and consequently predict a future downward trend. Suddenly you are not as satisfied as you were a moment ago.

Comparisonitis happens in three general areas of life experience— comparing what we have to what others have (possessions); comparing what we have accomplished to what others have accomplished (achievement); and comparing the way we are treated with the way we should be treated (expectations).

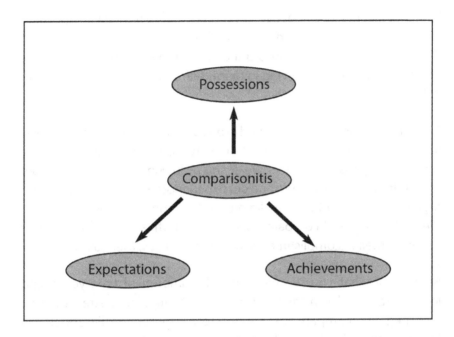

It is not possible to stop our survival instinct from constantly comparing our moment-to-moment experience with the past and future. Comparisonitis is automatic, it operates in non-conscious areas of the brain, and it cannot be switched off. But its adverse effects on quality of life can be moderated, and we will look at ways to do this.

**Comparisonitis—Possessions and Achievements.**

Marketers who appreciate the motivational power of these comparisons make a significant amount of money out of them. First, they sell us the idea (a very easy sell because instinct believes it) that doing well—having the newest, the best, the most expensive, and the most unique things— determines our value as a person and therefore our relative importance.

The speed of change in our lives means there are always emergent triggers for our instinct's fear of loss of importance. Just look at the 15 iPhone models Apple released from 2007 to 2017 or the new vehicle styles manufactured each year to see how companies easily capitalize on our compulsion to have the latest and the greatest.

From our instinct's perspective, we should update to remain important, even though we have a perfectly good working but out-of-date model. If we can't at this moment afford the upgrade, we are somehow not as good as we used to be. Giving in to this fear causes most of us to live in debt.

The genius of Facebook has cashed in on comparisonitis. Facebook makes it easy to spend large amounts of time attempting to gauge where we stand in comparison to others. We do this by looking at the listed number of friends others have, by posting our experiences and achievements, and organizing and inviting to make our profile more noticeable to others. We seek "likes" and compare ourselves with others by following their postings, their accomplishments, their experiences, their jokes.

Because of what you see there and the amount of time you spend looking, Facebook can create lots of dissatisfaction and distress through your negative comparisons. Yes, interest in others on Facebook can lead to satisfaction if you don't make any comparisons or when your comparisons are positive. But realize that comparisonitis is unconscious and ongoing, and it has a negative focus. Our unconscious comparisons are rarely positive. Facebook is time-consuming (and can be addictive) because your survival instinct motivates you to keep checking for any possible changes in your or your family's standing. If your status is currently positive, you must keep checking, hoping it stays that way. If it is negative, you have to keep checking with the hope that new postings (yours or others') will improve your relative importance and your perceived standing in your group.

**Comparisonitis—Expectations ("shoulds").**

Examples of comparisons between possessions and accomplishments are relatively easy to see in our daily lives. Keeping up with the Joneses—with their house, with their new car, with their holidays, with their new smart TV, with the success of their kids—is a readily recognized phenomenon.

Comparisons between what happens and what *should* happen, and how these comparisons affect our daily mood, are not as obvious. "Should" comparisons cause as much, if not more, distress than possession and achievement comparisons combined.

Simply put, you will automatically and naturally feel bad (or good) depending on whether the outcome of a comparison of how you are treated with the way you should be treated is negative (or positive). By automatic, I mean that your feeling will be instantaneous and will come before any conscious understanding of why.

You just feel bad (or good). Trying to make sense of how you feel without a consideration of instinct and comparisonitis will lead you to the conclusion that others must be responsible for how you feel. It seems that you were feeling OK before this. If you are now feeling upset, you must have been upset by your treatment or by what you saw on Facebook. The more you compare how you were treated with the way you deserve to be treated, the more your comparisons continue to upset you, and the more catastrophic the whole scenario becomes. Distress comes first and causes thinking to become negative. Negative thinking then magnifies distress, and the cycle repeats, potentially over and over.

As I write this, the US Open tennis tournament is on. A tournament winner is declared when a player has won more matches than anyone else. Each match is won by winning games, then sets, and with enough sets, the match. The outcome is decided only after a logical progression that starts with playing games.

Instinct does not work in this logical way. It acts in reverse. Based on unconscious triggers present at birth or unconscious triggers learned from the experience of growing up, instinct anticipates an outcome before any games are played, before anything has happened.

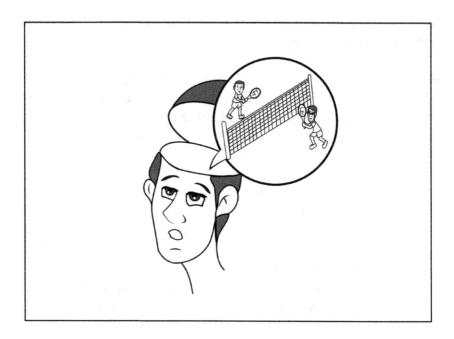

Once made, this determination causes us to feel bad (or good) and biases our conscious analysis in such a way to ensure that the instinctive outcome is justified. This bias has the potential to compromise our perception so much that we only see evidence to justify our feeling and may even see games won or lost that were never actually played. Instinct leads to a self-fulfilling prophecy.

"You didn't have to say it. I know what you were thinking" or "I know what you said, but you didn't mean it. What you really meant was ..."

If you do not realize the impact of instinct on your perceptions, your interpretation of the "games people play" will be so biased that you will believe that your feelings are caused by what other people do (or don't do). Once this bias makes you a victim, you constantly worry about others and what they think of you (comparisonitis). To overcome this anxiety, you will try to control them or convince yourself that the opinion of others doesn't matter, or you will blame them, or try to avoid them altogether.

The actual importance of any situation is mostly not relevant (e.g., a slow driver holding you up; someone leaving a trolley in the middle of the supermarket aisle while they choose the best bananas; someone talking loudly on their phone next you at the coffee shop; someone forgetting to thank you or forgetting your name or failing to invite you). So, arguing about what in fact happened is a waste of effort. According to your instinct, they did not do what they should have done. For your instinct, this difference is a survival concern—life-and-death—and therefore worthy of strong reactions and stewing (going over it repeatedly).

If at the time you had this experience something had already distressed you—like tiredness, illness, pain, previous history—then your sensitivity to the new scenario will be intensified by your existing frustration. This heightened sensitivity can lead you to the feeling that you just can't stand it. In this scenario, an emotional explosion may not be far away. We all have the potential to react very strongly to things of little consequence if our pre-existing frustration is particularly high.

"Should" comparisons have such a widespread impact on us, because they don't require a physical trigger. Being only thoughts, "shoulds" are potentially unlimited and can happen anywhere and anytime. You can suffer from "should" comparisonitis in the safety of your own home. While there is a physical limit to the number of possessions or achievements that incite comparisonitis, there is no limit to the number of "shoulds."

A mom says to her language-developing infant after passing her some fruit, "What do you say?"

Emily replies, "Tank do," and Mom responds with a cuddle.

Repeated occurrences of this scenario lead to the child's instinct determining that approval and security, comfort, and good feelings all go together. Offering something to another becomes a survival trigger, and "tank do" becomes a survival strategy.

A few years later, the child feels upset when someone (another child or adult) fails to acknowledge her gift or efforts to help.

"What's wrong, Emily?"

"Nothing," responds five-year-old Emily.

"What's wrong? Come on, tell me. It's all right."

Emily can't say what's wrong. At a conscious level, she doesn't know. Later, with more life experience, reasoning, and verbal skills, she might eventually say that she is upset because her friend Brook doesn't appreciate her effort to help her and she should. She always takes advantage of her, and she shouldn't.

Thirty years later, Emily gets angry at her husband, Nick.

"He never listens to me. I tell him repeatedly what he should do, but he never listens. But when his friend tells him the same thing, he hears it. His friend is more important than I am!"

Listening to "shoulds" in your own or others' thoughts is a way to spot comparisonitis. Reality testing the conclusions that we reach about how bad things are is a way to spot catastrophizing. Emily's comparisonitis is that Nick's friend is more important to Nick than she is. Catastrophizing will be covered in detail in the next chapter.

The topic of this angry outburst might have been about the importance of drinking enough water— not an immediate life-and-death scenario. However, Emily's instinct (unbeknownst to Emily) has assessed the issue as not being listened to, which has life-and-death significance. This assessment leads to conscious thoughts that catastrophize about Nick not valuing or loving her, about him leaving her because he obviously doesn't value her enough to listen to her, or about their children growing up without a father, their lives being ruined. These kinds of thoughts are just the tip of the iceberg when it comes to catastrophizing.

Nick's instinct (unbeknownst to Nick) also generates negative feelings that create a conscious thought spiral that is catastrophic. He has ideas of being treated like a child, getting no respect, and spending the rest of his life having to pander to a high-maintenance woman who doesn't credit him with the ability to make simple decisions like how much water to drink.

At an instinctive level, Emily's limbic system is telling her that her future security is at risk. This view generates conscious thoughts that she must be unimportant to Nick because he won't listen to her. Emily believes that Nick has upset her. But her instinctive rule about how she should be treated is the cause of her upset.

At an instinctive level, Nick's limbic system is telling him that his future relationship is at risk. This view generates conscious thoughts that Emily doesn't think he is competent enough to make sensible decisions, and this is a measure of her overall rating of him. Nick thinks that Emily upset him with her nagging. However, when Emily nags, the cause of his distress is his comparisonitis about how she should treat him better and shouldn't nag.

The conclusion reached through Emily's and Nick's "should" comparisons is that each has lost the approval of the other, and this causes instant, automatic, and natural distress for them both.

**Summary.**

- **Strong feelings are normal, natural reactions caused by your instinct's unconscious assessment of your situation.**
- **There is no off switch for instinct. We need to and will sweat the small, medium, and large stuff.**
- **Instinct creates strong feelings with excessive comparisons: comparisonitis.**
- **Recognition of your own comparisonitis gives you an opportunity to moderate its effects so you don't dwell on it.**
- **You can be happy despite unconscious comparisonitis.**

# CHAPTER 3
# CATASTROPHIZING

Homeostasis is a medical term describing the unconscious and automatic way the body keeps our organs operating within safe limits. Homeostasis is a medical example of the unconscious action of instinct keeping us safe. It is entirely focused on survival; it cares not how you feel. Sweating is unpleasant, but it is what it is. There is no avoiding it. Homeostasis works in the background of our life experience, and unless we are medically trained, we don't have any awareness that it is there, nor do we have any understanding of its complexity.

Excessive body temperature leads to organ malfunction and breakdown. Homeostasis regulates body temperature by sweating. Moisture on the skin has a cooling effect, and this helps to lower blood temperature and your body's temperature. You never sweat unless you need to. When you are hot, you cannot talk yourself out of sweating by telling yourself you are not. The more you focus on your sweating, the hotter you get.

**When you are sweating, your body temperature is high.
You should be sweating.**

Excessive muscle tension leads to muscle malfunction and threatens your survival. Working muscles require more oxygen and so your breathing rate increases. Your breathing rate never changes without your muscle tension changing. When you are tense, you cannot talk yourself out of breathing fast by telling yourself you are not tense. The more you focus on your tension, the more uptight you get.

**When you are breathing faster, your body is tense.
You should be breathing faster.**

Automatic, continual comparisons of the way your life is to the way it should be, keep you prepared to deal with threats to your survival. Your body uses feelings to enhance awareness, readiness, and to generate action. You cannot talk yourself out of feeling bad after your instinct has triggered these feelings. If you try to avoid these feelings, they get worse.

**When you are feeling bad, your survival is threatened.
You should be feeling bad.**

Okay, so you should be feeling bad, but for how long? Suppose it is possible to greatly reduce the length of time that you should be feeling bad. If so, you can be happy in spite of the necessary bouts of unhappiness that life throws at you.

If you are sweating too much, instinct doesn't push you to have surgery to remove your sweat glands. It wants you to get out of the sun or turn on the air conditioning. Focus on changing the causes, not the symptom, of being too hot (excessive sweating).

If you are breathing too fast, instinct does not want you to breathe slowly during physical exertion. It wants you to take a break from your physical exertion. Focus on changing the causes, not the symptom (rapid breathing).

If you are feeling bad when being threatened or being treated unfairly, instinct does not want you to be satisfied or happy. It wants you to do something to achieve safety or fairness. Focus on changing the causes, not the symptom (upsetness). In the case of feeling upset, you can try to reduce your distress by telling yourself to calm down and that everything works out all right in the end. This kind of common sense self-talk can help, but it won't help while you continue to feel bad.

Unless you first calm down, attempting to reduce distress by thinking differently won't work, because your instinct continues to catastrophize; it won't listen. Distress then gets worse as you realize your self-talk is not working. The fact is, you have to feel bad enough to dare to take the risk that may change your threatening situation.

From your instinct's perspective, feeling upset is a tool for survival. Feeling safe lowers your guard and your readiness for the next threat. You can't afford to feel safe and not worry. If you do, you are going to die happy. That might seem like a great way to go, except dying is not on the agenda for your instinct.

> **If instinct gets its way, the choice is between being alive and being happy.**
> **Instinct chooses survival.**

Being satisfied temporarily takes the focus off survival. For a while, you are not worrying, and you may fail to see or be prepared for the next threat that comes along. The experience of being unprepared when your guard was down has happened to most of us. Instinct operates on the principle that you stay ready by keeping your guard up. The effects of this influence on our conscious thoughts can be seen in urban wisdom like "Pride comes before a fall" and "Don't get a swelled head."

Over the last 70 years, efforts in cognitive behavioral psychology have endeavored to improve life experience—contentment, happiness, satisfaction—through strategies to increase the rationality and positivity of conscious thought. Although research results provide evidence of success in controlled situations, widespread use and assessment of these strategies outside of controlled experiments have not lived up to expectations. From a purely behavioral perspective, there is little to no evidence that human happiness in general has increased, or that the behavior of humans toward each other has improved. Add a threat to any situation, and human civility disappears. In fact, global news services and the internet might even give one the impression that human behavior has become unhappier, more discontent, and more violent.

In contrast to the limited success of 70 years of "gold standard" research in demonstrating the effectiveness of using conscious thought to improve feelings, the effective use of drugs to improve feelings has a history going back thousands of years. Throughout recorded human history, drugs have been used to change unhappiness, fear, and negativity into feelings of happiness, safety, and positivity. These drugs include alcohol, caffeine, nicotine, cocaine, sugar, cannabis, and a host of new synthetics (party drugs). They work, and they are robust—meaning they work in life-threatening situations. But the improvements they produce in mood are only temporary, and they have proved to have many side effects that actually reduce chances of survival. Drugs allow you to die happy.

It is because of their immediate effectiveness, availability, and affordability that drugs are so much of a problem. We have such a wide range of readily available legal and illegal drugs that are highly profitable for their makers and sellers. If we care to look, the ongoing influence of drugs is everywhere in our lives, our children's lives, our parent's lives, our friends' lives. The manipulation of feelings through drugs is now so pervasive (for example, sugar, alcohol, and a spiraling number of illegal drugs) that it is pointless trying to avoid mood-altering drugs.

An evolving theme in the widespread use of mood-altering drugs is the toxicity of the side effects of long-term or even short-term use. Weight gain (or loss), sleep dysfunction, cancers, immune system breakdowns, and inflammatory diseases are high on the list of the side effects of mood-altering drugs. For these drugs to improve feelings, they have to override the regulatory function of your survival instinct, which wants to keep you on edge, with your guard up, and on the lookout for any threat. To work, these drugs have to be potent in disrupting brain function. This disruption has an inflammatory effect on your immune system and makes it so much harder for your body to maintain homeostasis.

It is thought that because of the importance and complexity of effective homeostasis, its day-to-day workings need to be unconscious and automated in the brain. You don't need to observe or know about it. It does what it does automatically, and providing you don't get in its way, it works perfectly within the limitations of its capabilities and its resources.

But if you exceed its capability (take a powerful mood-altering drug) or compromise its resources (don't eat right or don't sleep enough)—or try to intervene and do it better—you threaten your own survival. If you think you know better, you are going to muck it up. Low mood, feeling discontent or unhappy, is a psychological version of homeostasis to grab your attention and get you focused on improving your circumstances. If you manage to free yourself of discontentment or unhappiness for too long, the psychological side of homeostasis runs out of motivation. You don't have to worry too much about this, however, because instinct makes sure that won't happen. As soon as the effects of the drug wear off, your unhappiness and discontent will return and possibly be worse after you (and others) condemn your drug-coping strategy.

**The sooner you realize that you naturally and normally need to feel bad on a regular basis, the sooner you will stop thinking something is wrong, accept it for what it is, start tolerating it better, and downgrade your response to feeling bad from a roadblock to a speed bump.**

You don't holler catastrophe whenever you sweat. It makes no sense to holler catastrophe whenever you feel bad. Feeling bad on a regular basis is necessary to keep you worrying, keep your guard up, and to motivate you into action the instant action is needed. Bad feelings naturally happen that cause you to take precautions in your life. When you start hollering about the fact that you feel bad and start to take avoidance action, your bad feelings will become more than a speed bump; they will become a road block. Your life bogs down and stops, stuck in discontentment and unhappiness.

Appreciate the fact that you sweat. It is necessary to keep you well and efficient when you are hot. Sweating some of the time doesn't mean that you will sweat all of the time. Appreciate the fact of your unhappiness and discontentment. It is necessary to keep you alert and ready for survival. Being unhappy and discontented some of the time doesn't mean you will be unhappy and discontented all of the time.

Opportunities for happiness and contentment occur as a result of the randomness of favorable life experience—providing you are open to it and aren't stuck in catastrophizing your current set of bad feelings.

There have been and will be many occasions when we feel dissatisfied or unhappy and can't see a logical reason for our distress. You might have achieved many of the things that you were told or believe are important for happiness in life, so you think you have no logical reason to feel bad.

Once aware of your own dissatisfaction, the negativity in your feeling distorts ongoing conscious thoughts.

Your dissatisfaction and frustration only gets worse, because you are thinking that you shouldn't be feeling this way. This is the point where you get stuck on your feelings. In trying to get unstuck, we take actions that make us even more stuck. We wrongly conclude that our negative beliefs and negative thoughts are the problem, and that changing negative thoughts into positive thoughts is the solution.

The origin of our negative feelings is our instinct's constant comparisonitis as it searches for survival signs and sources. As this comparison process operates in an area of the brain that we are unaware of, we do not realize it is happening. If we don't understand that instinct creates negative feelings through comparisonitis, we wrongly conclude that our negative feelings are the result of there being something wrong with us, our partner, our kids, our work, or friends.

These unhelpful conclusions start a *conscious* stream of thoughts looking for the things that have been and are bad about our life and about ourselves.

"I didn't try hard enough … I was treated so unfairly … I realize now that I made the wrong choices—school, work, partner, children, money."

"If I could just stop this negative thinking and try harder to be satisfied with things I do have and the achievements that I have made, I would be happy!"

> **The survival necessity of negativity at an instinctive level makes sure that dissatisfaction and unhappiness remain a part of life regardless of our beliefs, hope, and optimism and regardless of all our possessions, achievements, or recognition from others. Providing we can calm ourselves, thinking in useful ways when we do accomplish the things that are important to us extends our satisfaction and happiness, but this improvement was never meant to be permanent. Instinct wants to get distress and negativity going again as soon as possible to get our guard back up ready for the next threat to our survival.}**

Once you understand that the feeling of contentment and happiness is not meant to be permanent, you are on the way to being more open to favorable life experiences. You stop catastrophizing when you are feeling bad. You are realizing that it is natural to feel this way some of the time, and move from a stuck and narrow focus on how bad things are to an openness to external experiences where sources for new achievement and satisfaction lie. You also stop grieving when instinct reboots your mood of happiness back to its default survival mood of discontent. You have accepted that mood will change from happiness to unhappiness and back as regularly as sweating—that this is normal, natural, necessary, and unchangeable.

**Summary.**

- **Your survival instinct dictates that you will feel unhappy when you need to be alert to the possibility of threat.**
- **Acquired life experience and excessive comparisonitis can lead to instinctive false alarms.**
- **Accepting that neither unhappy or happy are meant to be permanent states reduces the negative impact of instinct on your moods.**
- **If you are not catastrophizing about feeling unhappy, you will be less frustrated, less likely to dwell on your unhappiness, and subsequently more open to happy events in your life.**

# CHAPTER 4
# FRUSTRATION

"Chicken Little" is a <u>folk tale</u> about a <u>chicken</u> who believes the world is coming to an end.

Chicken Little likes to walk in the woods. She likes to look at the trees. She likes to smell the flowers. She likes to listen to the birds singing.

One day, while she is walking, an acorn falls from a tree and hits the top of her little head.

"My, oh, my. The sky is falling. I must run and tell the lion about it," says Chicken Little, as she begins to run.

She runs and runs. By and by, she meets the hen.

"Where are you going?" asks the hen.

"Oh, Henny Penny, the sky is falling, and I am going to the lion to tell him about it."

"How do you know?" asks Henny Penny.

"It hit me on the head, so I know it must be so," says Chicken Little.

"Let me go with you!" says Henny Penny. "Run, run."

So, the two run and run until they meet Ducky Lucky.

"The sky is falling," says Henny Penny. "We are going to the lion to tell him about it."

"How do you know that?" asks Ducky Lucky.

"It hit Chicken Little on the head."

"May I come with you?" asks Ducky Lucky.

"Come," says Henny Penny.

So, all three of them run on and on until they meet Foxy Loxy.

"Where are you going?" asks Foxy Loxy.

"The sky is falling, and we are going to the lion to tell him about it," says Ducky Lucky.

"Do you know where he lives?" asks the fox.

"I don't," says Chicken Little.

"I don't," says Henny Penny.

"I don't," says Ducky Lucky.

"I do," says Foxy Loxy. "Come with me, and I can show you the way."

He walks on and on until he comes to his den.

"Come right in," says Foxy Loxy.

They all go in, but they never, never come out again.

In life-and-death situations, instinct is black-and-white, but its lack of flexibility in these moments is more than made up for by its blinding speed. Instinctive reactions are virtually instantaneous. Our survival instinct has evolved for situations where the speed of response is all-important. In survival situations, there is no time for conscious thought. If you think about it, you are dead.

Chicken Little is a story about instinct at work. It is also shows how instinct, without conscious intervention, can lead to unintended endings.

When instinct views circumstances as survival scenarios, it generates strong feelings to power its response. This brief experience, which ranges across the dimensions of pain or pleasure, is produced by the unconscious mental activity of comparisonitis, which compels us to compare with past accomplishments or with another's accomplishments to determine our relative importance. Instinct works on the principle that if you are noticed and have relative importance, you are valued and will be supported by the group. Without relative importance, you can't count on group support and are more vulnerable to threat. When comparisonitis results in an assessment of lowered relative importance, your instinct catastrophizes and turns this into a life-and-death scenario. Monitoring relative importance is an automatic daily task for us all because, from our instinct's perspective, relative importance is necessary for survival.

The feelings of pain or pleasure that are produced by comparisonitis— and intensified by catastrophizing—bias conscious thought. If the feeling is strong, its bias on conscious thought is powerful. When we are in psychological or physical pain, we only see the reasons we need to justify our feeling and action. When we are in pleasure, we only see the reasons we need to justify our feeling and action.

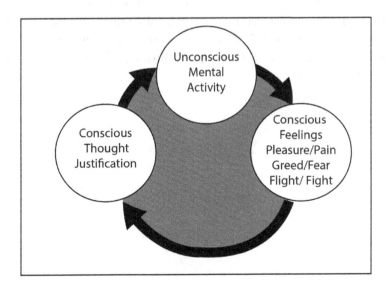

Research shows that emotion that originates in the unconscious limbic system in the brain registers split seconds before conscious thought registers in the frontal lobe of the brain.

Feelings of pleasure or pain occur before we have any understanding of what is happening. Feelings come first and bias our conscious thought and action. When intelligence, wisdom, experience, and common sense finally get going in our frontal lobe, their perspective has already been influenced by emotion, and their usefulness is undermined by the agitated state of Chicken Little, Henny Penny, and Ducky Lucky, who all agree that the sky Is falling. The biased conscious thought then further intensifies our experience of pain (or pleasure), which generates more biased opinions and so on. This circularity continues to support our biased interpretations, and the spiral effect is ongoing.

In the heat of the moment, when our feelings are running strong, our biased commitment to the rightness of our thinking and the justification of our actions is equally high. But when the intensity of our feelings subside, their bias on our thoughts weakens, and conscious logic and values get a chance to intervene. When our feelings subside, we often conclude that maybe we have overreacted and that our actions were not sensible or useful.

In the heat of the moment, we too often behave in ways that later we can't understand or accept and subsequently criticize ourselves for or put the blame on others. Rather than condemn ourselves or others for stupidity, it is far more useful to consider the idea that we have just spent time in the More-on Zone.

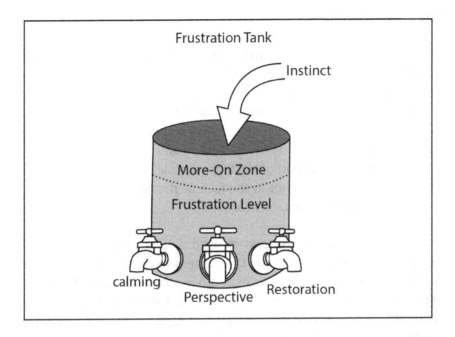

In the More-on Zone, the strength of our feelings focuses our attention so much on threat (or excitement) that we become tunnel-visioned. Chicken Little, Henny Penny and Ducky Lucky run so hard that they are immune to common sense, values, or logic. They fail to see the intentions of Foxy Loxy. The More-on Zone is so named to highlight the fact that although we are inclined to judge ourselves (or others) morons, we are not.

**In the More-on Zone, we are unable to be smart and sensible; we are not morons.**

Since the intensity of feeling in the More-on Zone can lead to behavior that momentarily we cannot control, it is important to accept the responsibility of staying out of the More-on Zone as much as possible. Managing this responsibility requires a model that provides an understanding of the process that slides us into the More-on Zone and importantly also shows us the steps we can take to halt or slow the slide.

**The Frustration Tank.**

The basic assumption of the Frustration Tank is that unconscious mental activity—comparisonitis and catastrophizing—causes an energizing feeling of agitation or arousal experienced as frustration. Frustration is used as a source of energy, and we store it in the tank to use now or later. Frustration can occur in both positive and negative situations. The following examples illustrate the frustration tank model with a focus on strong negative frustration: fight-or flight-arousal. But smart and talented people also do dumb things in the face of strong positive frustration: greed, excitement and attraction arousal.

Instinct is a compulsive process of unconscious mental activity that compares our accomplishments to another's to determine our relative importance and hence our chances of survival. From its point of view, the threat (or opportunity) for survival lies in the detection of change. The focus of comparisonitis is on what is different, what was different, what could be different. When instinct registers difference at an unconscious level, one of its goals is to generate feelings to make sure we notice the difference. It has to generate feelings strong enough to grab our attention, because at a conscious level our attention tunes out things that are constant.

For example, if you live or work around constant noise, you cease to notice it after a while, at least until it stops. The house that I grew up in was at the bottom of a hill on a major road close to the center of Brisbane, with a tram stop right in front of the house—constant background traffic/people noise. On the occasions when my family did get away on holiday, I could not sleep for the first few nights because it was too quiet; something wasn't right. After a few nights, I got used to it and slept well. When we returned from holiday, I could not sleep for the first few nights because it was too noisy; something wasn't right. After a few nights, I got used to the noise and returned to sleeping well.

The Frustration Tank model is important to help draw attention to the fact that we live with constant frustration. Life makes sure of that. Because of its constancy, we have tuned it out, and we only notice the effect it has on us when it gets severe. We tend not to be aware of just how our frustration accumulates, and therefore are not prepared for the suddenly heightened sensitivity we can have to everyday events. Others may see evidence of our accumulated frustration when we do not. If our frustration reaches a high enough level, we enter the More-on Zone. When this occurs, the agitation triggered by even a very minor event can create a reaction of extreme survival behavior that for a short time is beyond conscious control. At this moment smart, talented, and good people do dumb and awful things.

If we have tuned out our existing frustration level, if we are unaware of just how frustrated we are, we will be surprised by the suddenness and intensity of our feelings and reactions. We will also be surprised at having them in response to minor causes of frustration. When we respond suddenly and strongly to minor things, we (and others) might conclude that there is something very wrong with us (we're morons). Alternatively, we might also justify the intensity of our reaction by deciding that there is something very wrong with others.

Let's take a closer look at the Frustration Tank model.

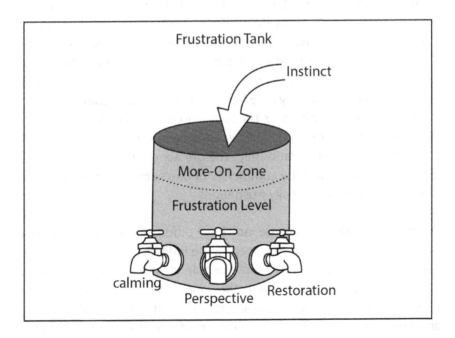

The model assumes we all have this tank, much like all cars have gas tanks (or, for electric cars, a battery). The tank contains accumulated frustration produced by comparisonitis in response to our daily experience. Frustration is accompanied by physiological arousal that can be pleasant (excitement) but mostly unpleasant (agitation, worry, anger). Unconscious mental activity—comparisonitis—continually inputs frustration into the tank (you can experience frustrating dreams even when you are asleep). The volume of incoming frustration depends on your life circumstances (what has happened, what is happening, what might happen). It depends on the amount and complexity of your comparisonitis (unconscious mental activity) and on the amount and complexity of your associated conscious thoughts. This physiological agitation or arousal will then bias conscious thoughts, intensify feelings, and energize survival behavior.

A person with narrow life experience of threatening events (e.g., a child, or a "civilian") will have a less well-developed survival instinct than a person with a wider experience of threatening events (e.g., a police officer, EMT or paramedic, a firefighter, or someone in the Armed Forces).

A child's survival instinct (comparisonitis) becomes more complex because of the experiences they have growing up in their family and going to school. A civilian's survival instinct becomes more complex as a result of life experience after joining a force (e.g., a police force). The life experience and comparisonitis of most teenagers are less than that of an adult and explain why they feel so sure about what they know and what their parents don't know. The comparisonitis of an adult not having experienced a long-term relationship becomes more complex as a result of their first long-term relationship. The greater the complexity of one's experience, the greater the complexity of one's comparisonitis and the greater the potential for daily frustration.

Differences in life events cause individual differences in the experience of daily frustration. There also seem to be individual differences in the size of the tank, meaning that some people seem to tolerate frustration better than others. But to keep the model simple, we will concern ourselves more about what we can modify (i.e., the volume of incoming and existing frustration), instead of the size of the tank, which is probably a genetic trait and can't be modified.

Looking again at the tank, you will observe a marked level near the top that indicates the entrance to the More-on Zone. When frustration moves above this line, it triggers reflexive survival reactions that are extreme and very resistant to the moderation of conscious logical thought. In the More-on Zone, Chicken Little, Henny Penny, and Ducky Lucky have tunnel vision and don't listen.

In the More-on Zone, there is *more going on* in the experience of agitation or arousal than we can manage. We lose conscious control. Our feelings and actions (fight or flight) are taken over by our instinct for survival.

**The moment the More-on Zone is entered is the moment when there is more on us than we can tolerate or handle.**

I was attending a school party being held in the parking lot of my child's primary school when a three-year-old riding a plastic horse on wheels lost control and began rolling down the steep entrance to the lot. At the bottom of that was a busy road. Three adults, including myself, took off running after the child. We were all too late, in that we caught the child on the horse at the same moment, but none of us could stop from running full pelt out into the road with the child and the plastic horse. On this occasion, there were no oncoming cars or trucks. There could have been. It was only after my heart stopped racing and my breathing settled a little that I realized that the only focus that all of us had as we ran down the entrance and into the road was catching the child before he got hurt. All of us could have run into the path of oncoming traffic.

In this case, instinctive behavior was not self-centered; it was focused on the child's survival—on the survival of the species. But this is unusual. Instinctive behavior is mostly self-centered. It has an intense, narrow, here-and-now focus (no consideration for what's next) with the goal of surviving the moment. When it is focused on the self, it allows no compassion or respect for others. Most of the time when you are in the More-on Zone, you are toxic to other people and, in the long run, toxic to yourself. Many people fleeing the scene of a catastrophe are in the More-on Zone. They will trample others to survive and will suffer later from the post-traumatic stress of having survived when others didn't.

At the bottom of the tank, you can see some taps. Since comparisonitis creates a constant incoming flow of frustration into the tank, and since you want to stay out of the More-on Zone as much as possible, having a way to regulate the level of frustration in the tank is important.

The three taps represent the three kinds of activity aimed at managing frustration levels by:

- Step 1. Reducing the intensity of feelings **(calming)**.
- Step 2. Becoming aware of instinctive comparisonitis and catastrophizing **(Perspective)**.
- Step 3. Deliberate intent and action to respond to your situation despite how you feel **(Restoration)**.

Specific examples of the use of these taps are given in Chapter 7.

**Step 1: Calming.**

In the heat of the moment Chicken Little, Henny Penny, and Ducky Lucky are on the run. The sky is falling. Arousal and agitation are intense, and repeatedly saying so makes it worse. In the heat of the moment, everything is black or white, and your common sense is really dumbed down. You have to release the intensity of your feelings before you do anything else.

**In the heat of the moment, conscious thinking—talking sense to yourself—will not work as a first step.**

Unconscious pattern matching in the limbic system—comparisonitis—has freaked out Chicken Little and crew, and they are off and running in tunnel-vision mode. Instinct is in survival mode. The pressure is on, and feelings and behavior have already occurred before any conscious thought. Effective tank management will require deliberate, sensible thought, but only after the pressure of agitation has been eased.

**Initially, feelings come before thought, so work on feelings first.**

Physical activity powered by the energy of your agitation can provide brief relief that will release some of the pressure to survive and lower the frustration level in your tank. It is almost too late to talk sense to yourself if you are already on the edge of the More-on Zone. You need to do something to ease the intensity of your arousal, but unless the activity produces immediate relief, it will add to your frustration.

All activities are not equal. Some are better or worse than others regarding the relief they provide. Activities that work quickly and that don't cause significant medium to long-term dissatisfaction are the ideal activities. But we don't need to find ideal activities, just active ones. Any physical activity that releases tension and produces immediate relief works well to reduce the intensity of an instinctive survival reaction. However, this is only true if the frustration of achieving the release does not cancel out the brief satisfaction of the release. For example, drinking, gambling, or spending are activities that reliably produce brief satisfying outcomes like relaxation or excitement but that over time can have high frustration costs because of the negative impact on your relationships, your work, and your family.

Activity in the form of any movement works well to soak up agitation and produce brief relief. Physical activities that have low initial frustration, like fiddling, doodling, and tapping, are good choices. If you are built for it, physical exercise is a better choice, even though at first the brief satisfaction it provides might be outweighed by the frustration of the sweat and effort to get going. However, the more you exercise, the better the balance between frustration and satisfaction will be. As you get fitter, the frustration of starting will reduce significantly. If you get to the point of moving long enough on any one occasion, usually over twenty minutes, you will experience the good feeling that you get from the endorphins your body produces in response to your movement.

Effective use of movement requires a deliberate allocation of activity time on a regular basis. The activity will have to be effective in the sense that the immediate satisfaction it provides makes the immediate tension and frustration of starting the activity worthwhile. There are 168 hours in every week. You might sleep eight hours a night, which leaves 112 hours every week. Out of these remaining 112, hours you need to allocate four to six hours a week for physical activity. Taking approximately 5 percent of your awake time to assist in managing the level of frustration in your tank is not selfish. It is arguable that failing to take this time is being selfish, in that failure to do so means that you expose your family, coworkers, and friends more often to your More-on Zone.

**Step 2: Perspective.**

In this step, you consciously work to become aware that your strong feelings are being caused by comparisonitis and catastrophizing *about* your situation, rather than being caused *by* your situation. Recognizing that your perspective of the situation is more important than the situation itself is essential for effective management of ongoing frustration. Remember, you have to lower the initial intensity of your feelings before you can achieve and use perspective.

The goal of perspective is to bring your attention to the "sky is falling" nature of your survival instinct. You need to picture your survival instinct madly running around to ensure your survival. You need to acknowledge its effort as being in your best interest and thank it for doing its job— to keep you alive. If you can "normalize" the catastrophizing nature of instinct, you will be more likely to see that it is distressing you with exaggerated interpretations, and therefore be in a better position to cope in spite of it.

In Step 2, you are identifying the instinctive causes of your feelings and acknowledging that intensity is caused by comparisonitis and catastrophizing, not by the situation.

**Step 3: Restoration.**

In this step, a conscious effort is required to convince yourself that the intensity of your feelings is not confirmation of a real survival threat— that the intensity is not justified on this occasion. It is this effort that marks the onset of resilience. Resilience is the ability to interpret your experience in a way that motivates you to do something useful. If the intensity of your feelings is interpreted to mean that now is the time to improve your situation—rather than now is the time to die—then you will likely do something useful. In resilience mode, you are normalizing the intensity of your instinctive reactions as natural but not appropriate to your circumstances. You also remind yourself that you can tolerate the intense feelings that you are having and still respond effectively in spite of them.

After you have started some activity to release the initial intensity in your feelings, you use resilience to keep the activity going by aiming to increase the satisfaction it produces. You could think:

"Sure it's hot today, and walking is a sweaty activity, but it's not so bad and, hey, well worth the great feeling I get afterwards. I need to walk to calm down."

After reviewing your values and goals as a compass for what you are going to do next, resilient thought also helps to motivate and firm up your intent to take action:

"Cleaning the cupboard (gardening, playing the guitar, jogging) does make me feel better, and that makes me better at everything I do. I can go clean the cupboard even if I don't feel like it. I can tolerate it; it's not so bad. I'll be getting something done, and after a few minutes, I will want to keep going. I will feel less frustrated then and will be ready to have another go at managing my comparisonitis and catastrophizing."

Restoration needs to include thought that motivates action. It is not enough to rely on the idea that "Every cloud has a silver lining" or "Every problem is an opportunity." Restoration has to include concrete things to do to uncover or create the silver lining or the opportunity.

The issue of belief has been a controversial one in the study of resilience. Do you have to believe, really believe, resilient thought for it to generate action and potential satisfaction? There is no definitive research to address this question, mostly because there is no agreement on how to go about measuring belief. Is belief two-dimensional? Do you either believe or not believe? Or is belief multidimensional? Are there degrees of believing?

Perhaps the most accepted view on restoration and belief is that if you put effort into creating resilient thought, then whether you entirely believe it doesn't matter. If your values, logic, and common sense tell you that it is useful to assure yourself that gardening will put you in a mood to try again in your difficult situation—and if self-talk tells you what to do to better prepare yourself for trying again—then deliberately telling yourself this over and over will decrease your frustration and increase your confidence in the short term. But only as long as you actively remind yourself. Resilient thought requires self-talk for it to work.

If you get knocked down by your feelings, how do you get up again? Restoration requires risk-taking and learning from consequences. Responsible risk-taking requires you to evaluate the possible consequences of your actions before you perform them—to assess the positives and negatives of the risk. Effective risk-taking requires you to work up the courage to take the risk; to have in place strategies to tolerate the anxiety associated with your actions; to measure the outcome of the risk; to modify what you do next'; and to be willing to repeat the process.

Action learning also requires a definition of success and means of objective measurement of progress. It encourages a focus on developing the skills needed for success, on the motivation to practice these skills, and an openness to change in the face of objective evidence.

**Summary.**

- **Instinct keeps us safe but also has the potential to keep us unhappy.**
- **To be safe and happy, we need to manage calming, perspective, and restoration—these steps must be followed in order.**
- **Reducing the intensity of your feelings can stop you dwelling on them.**
- **Awareness of your comparisonitis and catastrophizing gives you a perspective to talk sense to yourself.**
- **Get out of the More-on Zone before you try talking sense to yourself.**
- **Restoration requires the ability to interpret your experience in a way that motivates you to do something useful and then to follow through.**
- **Restoration requires action.**

# CHAPTER 5
# SATISFACTION

"(I Can't Get No) Satisfaction" is a song released in 1965 by the English rock band The Rolling Stones. It was written by Mick Jagger and Keith Richards and produced by Andrew Loog Oldham and became the band's first No. 1 single.

In the song, the lyrics complain that no matter how hard Mick tries, he can't get no satisfaction. He can't get it from the radio, because the radio provides useless information. He can't get it from the TV, because the presenter smokes the wrong kind of cigarettes. He can't get it from a relationship, because he is in a depressed frame of mind. He keeps trying and trying and trying, but he *can't get no satisfaction*. Jagger said in an interview, after the massive success of the song, that the lyrics represented his view of the world, his frustration with everything.

It was hugely successful because it tapped into and provided an outlet for the underlying pain instinct causes us in its drive to keep us alive.

One of the most unhelpful ideas about happiness is the seemingly logical idea that one's life has to be full of purpose and the satisfaction of achievement for you to be happy.

The reality of our life experience is that we often struggle with knowing what our purpose is or should be. Things just happen that give our life purpose, and other things just happen that take that meaning away and provide us with a new purpose or direction. Many of us have experienced periods of having a clear sense of purpose and periods where there seemed to be no purpose or point to life. Some of us have never experienced a time of having a clear sense of purpose, and a very few of us have always had a clear sense of purpose and direction in life.

However, the fact is, during intervals of pursuing a clear direction or purpose, we have been both happy and unhappy. Likewise, during intervals of being without purpose and being a bit aimless, we also have had moments of being happy and unhappy, though it is admittedly easier to remember the unhappy times.

Meaning or purpose does give direction and provides a compass for day-to-day efforts. However, having a direction is not a requirement for happiness or a guaranteed shield against unhappiness. You don't have to know the meaning of life, you don't have to have goals, and you don't have to wake up to each day mapped out with milestones to reach and lists to complete. You might be in a period in your life where you are full of purpose, and if so, your activity level will be higher than if you are in an aimless period. But an increased level of activity does not only mean increased opportunities for happiness. It also means increased opportunities for unhappiness. If you are in an aimless period of life where there seems to be no point, your activity level will be lower. A lower level of activity does mean decreased opportunities for happiness. But it also means decreased opportunities for unhappiness.

The point is that it when it comes to happiness, it does not matter what period of life you are in right now. A key to being happy in spite of yourself is to accept that right now your life circumstances are the way they are, and they do not need changing. If you want to change them, go ahead. If they are toxic, it is worthwhile putting effort into improving them. However, if changing your life circumstances is not possible now or ever, they don't need to be changed for you to be happy.

Not all, but many of the circumstances we find ourselves in are beyond our ability to change. It is arguable that we can't know if we don't try. But the choice to try or not try is not causally related to happiness. We can be happy whether we try or not.

**Origins of Satisfaction.**

Unconscious mental processes with the goal of survival determine the level of satisfaction we get from any activity. How could an infant get satisfaction from biting or hitting another child that is taking their toy, or from taking the other kid's food, or throwing their own food on the ground, or breaking their own toy, or ripping a page out of their own book? From a logical, value-driven perspective, there is no way a child should get satisfaction from these actions. But infants and children and also adults do things like this and do show evidence of feeling satisfied with themselves—until they get in trouble. Getting in trouble eventually eliminates this instinctive behavior from their repertoire, at least for the time being.

Instinct drives the infant, child, teenager, adult, and older adult to be noticed and valued because that's where security lies. As the process is unconscious, we can be surprised by how much satisfaction or dissatisfaction we can feel in new situations. When this happens, we can't say why we feel the way we feel; we just do. As our life experience increases, we become more able to explain our behavior—and perhaps increasingly prejudiced in our explanations.

Life experience of what is satisfying and what is not helps us to choose new activities to experience satisfaction. Learning from experience makes sense. But life experience can also be a hindrance when looking for new satisfying activities. It is easy to make the mistake that, based on prior experience, we won't like something that we have never tried only because an instinctive comparison has linked it to another activity that we didn't like.

Generalizations are made about what people find satisfying—to eat, to work, to be loyal, to be responsible. If you want to work on your happiness, you have to go beyond generalizations and discover your individuality in what you find satisfying. Generalizations can limit the degree of openness in your personal search and bias your willingness only toward particular types of activity:

"You shouldn't put work before your family; you shouldn't put your kids before your partner or your partner before your kids; you shouldn't put your passion before your responsibilities."

Conscious perspectives can help with the choice of a satisfying activity, but don't let them prevent you from trying something new.

The achievement of satisfaction does not require you to have a clear sense of purpose. If you are not getting enough satisfaction in your life, an aimless search for more can work as long as it opens you up to new experiences.

**The Satisfaction Tank.**

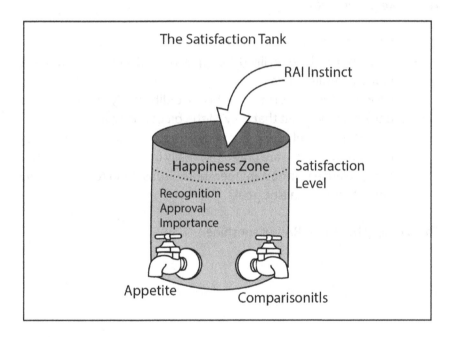

The human survival instinct has learned that safety, security, and group support comes from:

- Being recognized by the group.
- Being approved of by the group.
- Being considered relatively important by the group.

The underlying assumption of the Satisfaction Tank is that when you are recognized, when you receive approval, or when you are treated as if you are relatively important, survival instinct registers these conditions as safe and generates satisfaction. Satisfaction does not require all three of these conditions to be present, but the strength of satisfaction will be affected by the number that are present.

The impact of these conditions on your life and happiness is one of the key points of this book. I want to introduce an abbreviation for these conditions to make it easier for you to read as I refer to them often. I also want to use an abbreviation that will also serve as a memory hook to help you remember these conditions.

The abbreviation is RAi.

- R for recognition (being noticed).
- A for approval (being liked, being respected, being encouraged, being complimented).
- i for relative importance (This is deliberately a small "i" to underline the point that only a little bit of importance is enough for instinct to feel supported and secure. Instinct has learned that in any group, there are only a few really important members but many relatively important members. So, aspiring to be relatively important is a realistic goal.)

The memory hook is a "RAi" of sunshine.

What your instinct wants and needs to survive is a RAi of sunshine. Satisfaction is a product of RAi. The quality of RAi determines the motivational strength of the satisfaction.

Like frustration, satisfaction is a source of motivation. Frustration motivates through the power of agitation and pain; it uses the "stick" approach. Satisfaction motivates through pleasure; it uses the "carrot" approach.

We store satisfaction and the RAi it contains for use now or later. As the satisfaction level in the tank rises, we eventually enter the Happiness Zone. This zone marks the level of satisfaction we require to experience happiness. We don't get there very often because there are many things making it difficult for satisfaction to reach this level and making it hard to remain there. We have only limited influence over new satisfaction. Variables that affect incoming RAi include things we can't control in our environment:

- Our natural talent or ability.
- Our instinct's comparisonitis and catastrophizing.

- Luck.

and things we can influence or control like:

- Opportunity.
- Our level of skill.
- Mastery and resilience.

We also have limited influence over how long the satisfaction lasts. Factors that affect how quickly we use up the RAi of stored satisfaction include things like our instinct's appetite—how needy it is for ongoing recognition, approval, and relative importance.

---

**Hungry Hombre.**

**Childhood experience mostly determines the hunger or neediness of instinct. A child who regularly and consistently received RAi had no instinctive need to save it for a rainy day. For this child, RAi and the security it provided was readily available. On the other hand, the experience of a child who received little RAi, or who received RAi inconsistently, shaped a survival instinct that hungers for RAi. This hunger leads to an adult who is high maintenance, always seeking attention and reassurance, and never being satisfied with RAi, because he or she has learned that RAi is always inconsistent. This adult is both needy for RAi and vulnerable to being manipulated by RAi.**

---

Pharmacology uses the term half-life to describe the period required for the effect of a drug on the body to be reduced by one-half. The half-life of a drug is a measure of how long its effects last. If we use half-life to measure how long the effects of feelings last, instinct ensures that the half-life of positive feelings is much shorter than the half-life of negative feelings. Positive feelings relax and drop your guard, whereas negative feelings agitate and keep you alert. For people without specific training (that's most of us), survival in real life-and-death situations depends upon the intensity of the negative feelings of fear, anger, and hate. Survival requires that our frustration lasts a lot longer than our satisfaction.

However, if we deliberately intervene, we can increase the half-life of our satisfaction by consciously generating RAi.

Most of us have had the experience of satisfaction from an accomplishment or unexpected good luck. If you reflect on these occasions, you will observe that no matter how great the satisfaction, there was soon a sense of anti-climax. The satisfaction didn't last for very long, certainly not as long as you expected. You may have been briefly happy, but it wasn't a key to unending happiness. Satisfaction fades over time, over a very short time. Momentary satisfaction and even happiness can come from accidentally doing the right thing, in the right place, at the right time. However, it takes deliberate effort to achieve ongoing satisfaction and more frequent periods of happiness. Maybe you can't make your luck, but you can generate RAi and make your satisfaction. And if you work at it enough, you can get yourself, at least briefly, into the Happiness Zone on a regular basis.

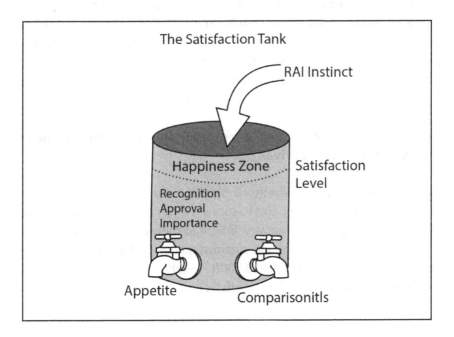

Let's take a closer look at the Satisfaction Tank model. The function of the tank is to collect and accumulate the satisfaction resulting from the RAi of positive random environmental events—luck, from favorable comparisonitis, and deliberate efforts to generate RAi. Satisfaction generates physiological arousal that is reassuring, relaxing, and to some extent confidence-building. The rate of RAi coming into the tank depends on your life circumstances (what has happened, what is happening, what might happen); it depends on the amount and complexity of your comparisonitis and on the amount and complexity of your deliberate plans and actions. The physiological comfort experienced when satisfied automatically biases conscious thoughts toward more positive plans and action that lead to the potential of more incoming satisfaction.

Looking again at the tank, you will observe a marked level up near the top of the tank that denotes the entrance to the Happiness Zone. When satisfaction moves above into this zone, Chicken Little, Henny Penny, and Ducky Lucky are extremely tolerant of falling acorns. From an instinctive, big-picture perspective, this is hazardous to survival. A chilled-out instinct is a sluggish instinct. In the Happiness Zone, contentment is high, frustration sources have been filtered out, and the level of frustration in the Frustration Tank is low. Low frustration eases agitation, facilitates contentment, and lowers mental and physical alertness. Happiness is a place of contentment; it is not a place that stimulates mental and physical activity. When we are happy, we don't need creativity, problem-solving, or alertness. We feel safe.

**When the Happiness Zone is entered, the associated drop in alertness is a risk to survival.**

We don't need to debate whether it is worth risking survival to be happy, or whether there is even a point to survival if you are not happy, because happiness is only ever temporary. Inherited mental and physical ability, childhood events, changing life circumstances—including opportunity and luck—contribute to the 84,000 variables that influence daily incoming RAi and the half-life of satisfaction.

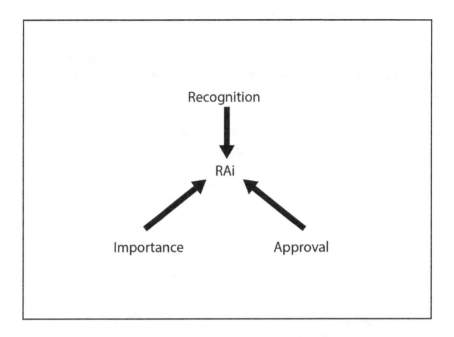

At the bottom of the tank, there are two significant outlets for accumulating satisfaction. One of these is your instinct's appetite for recognition, approval, and relative importance. When your environment fails to provide adequate recognition, approval, and relative importance, your instinct feeds on stored satisfaction to provide the RAi it needs to feel safe. The other major outlet is comparisonitis: continuous automatic comparisons of how you feel today compared to yesterday and how you think you will feel tonight and tomorrow. Comparisonitis anticipates and looks for negative change and for what could go wrong. The frustration caused by comparisonitis dilutes RAi and turns satisfaction into dissatisfaction.

We can be happy more of the time if we take conscious action to increase and preserve the RAi accumulating in our Satisfaction Tank. If we don't do this, our survival instinct's increasing need for RAi as we age will result in chronically low levels of satisfaction in the tank and continue to lower the quality of our overall life experience.

Any situation can be measured along a difficulty dimension to determine the level of associated frustration and along a RAi dimension to determine the level of derived satisfaction. The Frustration Tank and Satisfaction Tank models are related to each other in that they measure variables important in the overall experience of life and happiness. Frustration and satisfaction are in a see-saw relationship with each other. As frustration goes up, the value of associated satisfaction goes down. As satisfaction goes down, the possibility of happiness diminishes. As frustration goes down, the value of associated satisfaction goes up. As satisfaction goes up, so does the potential to be happy.

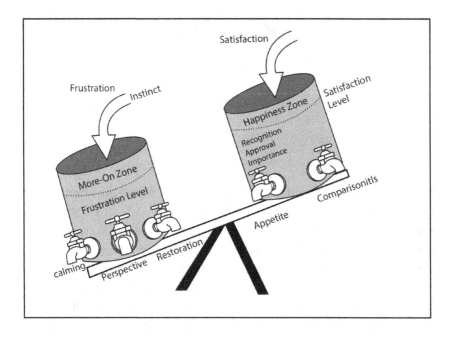

It is useful to understand the happiness potential in our lives from both the frustration and satisfaction perspectives. Being able to work on frustration and satisfaction gives us two avenues to address our instinctive needs, to lessen the intensity of what we feel, and to modify the actions we subsequently take. It is also useful to think about happiness in terms of the balance between frustration and satisfaction. If the satisfaction you feel in any situation outweighs the frustration of the situation, you have the potential to be happy, provided you can hang on to your RAi long enough. Under these conditions, happiness can be more frequent, but it will never be permanent. Instinct makes sure of this.

**It is what it is, and it doesn't have to change.**

The "it" in this statement refers to your present circumstances:

- Whether you have purpose in life.
- Whether you have a job.
- Whether you are in love.
- Whether you are a parent.
- Whether your kids are doing well.
- Whether you have friends.
- Whether you are succeeding.

These things are important but not necessary for your happiness. You can be happy with or without them.

**Happiness is not determined by your life circumstances, or by your achievements, or by what you have or don't have. Happiness is an emotional state determined by the balance between satisfaction and frustration. If satisfaction outweighs frustration, you will be happy more frequently. How long you stay happy depends on your instinct's ongoing need for RAi.**

**Dimensions of Satisfaction—Now and Then.**

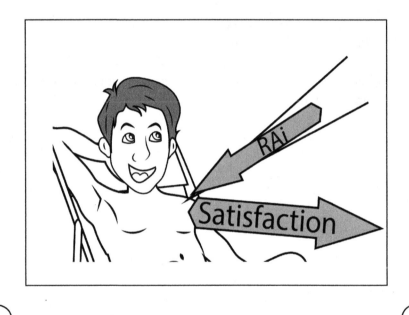

Comparisonitis mostly dilutes RAi, but occasionally increases RAi. By its very nature, there is a time-traveling element involved with comparisons that generate two types of satisfaction—now compared with now and now compared with then (either a past then or a future then).

When we compare the RAi we feel now, with how we want to feel now, or how we should feel now, we are experiencing *now satisfaction*.

When we compare the RAi we feel now with the RAi we felt yesterday or with the level of RAi we expect to feel tomorrow, we are experiencing *then satisfaction*.

You need to be aware of these two different types of satisfaction to understand how it is possible to feel dissatisfied when you seemingly have no reason to be. You think now should be satisfying because you are succeeding, winning, achieving, and having all that you want. So why aren't you satisfied? The answer is because, unbeknownst to you, your instinct is catastrophizing about the difference between what you have now and what you had yesterday or what you expect to have tomorrow.

When you do experience a situation where satisfaction outweighs frustration, you have the potential to feel happy and contented. This won't last, though. If you expect this, you can do something about it, and you can increase the length of your happy feeling.

From your instinct's perspective, contentment is a threat to your survival because your guard drops. Instinct works to keep you alert to the possibility of a threat by making sure that satisfaction, once achieved, doesn't last for long. From your instinct's perspective, the moment you feel satisfied marks the onset of increased vulnerability. So, once you are satisfied, instinct kicks in with comparisonitis to gradually undermine your satisfaction and contentment to get your guard up, to get you ready for threats and to maximize your chances to survive.

So, once you are satisfied, you want to consciously re-focus attention on the RAi you are enjoying. Celebrate your RAi. Happiness is a feeling experienced any time when the feeling of satisfaction reaches your Happiness Zone. Happiness will last longer if you can keep your satisfaction at this level.

One day, I was waiting to collect my daughter after school. Parked near a pedestrian crossing regulated by lights, I watched a couple of approximately ten-year-old kids pressing the button to stop the traffic. When the traffic stopped, they didn't cross. Instead, they waited until the traffic started moving again and then pressed the button again—and again.

They seemed to get a great deal of RAi out of being able to stop the traffic in such an easy way—just by pressing a button. Small effort (little frustration) was required to press the button to get the great satisfaction of being able to control the traffic. They were happy doing this until a teacher came along and spoke to them very sternly. The frustration of being chewed out lowered their satisfaction, and they dropped out of the Happiness Zone. For these two normal kids, the situation had changed. Pressing the button was still easy, but it was now a source of frustration greater than satisfaction as a result of getting in trouble from teacher intervention. The situation was no longer worth it, at least while a teacher or parent was looking.

Instinct is trying to ensure that satisfaction and happiness are temporary. It uses comparisonitis and catastrophizing to make this happen. Comparisonitis focused on the frustration and satisfaction of any activity will sooner or later increase frustration and lower satisfaction. At this point, we catastrophize, and there goes our feeling of happiness.

Complete this sentence: "*I am happy when* _____"

Or "*I am satisfied when* _____"

Or "*I am content when* _____"

Or "*I am relaxed when* _____"

Suppose you thought, "I am happy when I am watching my kids play" or "I am content when I am relaxing with my partner" or "I am satisfied when I am cycling well" or "I am relaxed when I am working" or "I am happy when I am not working."

All it takes for you to lose the feeling of happiness in any of these situations is anything that either changes the frustration of the activity or anything that changes the RAi coming from the activity—or both (most likely).

Introduce circumstances like tiredness, sickness, physical pain, competition, or risk, and the frustration of the effort increases.

"It's too hard, harder than I expected, or harder than it should be!"

As this happens, comparisonitis easily makes it worse by making you frustrated with your frustration and dissatisfied with your dissatisfaction. Comparisonitis achieves its results through unconscious mental activity. This unconscious mental activity generates bad feelings that then bias conscious thought like:

"I should get more sleep. It's unfair that I can't get more sleep."

"I should be managing the pain better. It's unfair that I have this pain."

"I used to be more competitive. I used to be able to take risks."

"I should be enjoying this more. This used to make me happy."

"What's wrong with me?"

You offset this unconscious process by generating your own RAi. But note that activities that produce RAi today can be a cause of frustration in the future if the activity has negative consequences (drugging, spending, gambling, gossiping, complaining, undermining, avoiding, over-exercising, over/under-eating, etc.).

So, when it comes to choosing specific activities in search of RAi, it helps to think ahead. While none of us has a crystal ball, we all have life experience that allows us to join the dots between our actions and consequences. If you speed, you will be fined sooner or later. If you treat people badly, eventually they may treat you badly. If you treat people well, sooner or later they may treat you well.

However, thinking and planning will not protect you from the potential future deterioration of RAi you will get from any activity. Thinking ahead can lessen negative outcomes, but it can't prevent the value of positive outcomes deteriorating, as in the end instinct uses comparisonitis to put you back on edge and keep your guard up.

It is what it is. If you accept this reality, you will catastrophize less about it and be better placed to take responsibility to continue generating RAi and happiness in spite of it.

Comparisonitis is a normal reaction to everyday circumstances. It is very helpful to expect and accept it as you would expect and accept sweating when it is hot, or breathing hard when you are exercising. It is going to happen; it is what it is.

Satisfaction will occur more of the time if you can accept that when you do get it, it isn't supposed to last for very long. It is normal that whatever you have is never enough. Instinct makes it so. But despite this, you can get some *satisfaction*. "Hey, hey, hey!"

**Summary.**

- **Clarity of purpose is not necessary for happiness. You can be happy even if you are aimless.**
- **RAi is an abbreviation for recognition, approval, and relative importance.**
- **The RAi we get from any activity determines the amount of satisfaction we feel.**
- **In situations where RAi is scarce, instinct uses accumulated satisfaction to provide the RAi it needs to feel supported and safe.**
- **Comparisonitis dilutes RAi and can turn satisfaction into dissatisfaction.**
- **As we grow older, our need for RAi also grows.**
- **Diminished or erratic RAi in childhood leads to an adult needy for RAi and vulnerable to being manipulated by providers of RAi.**
- **Happiness reflects the see-saw relationship between frustration and satisfaction.**
- **If you work at it, you can get yourself into the Happiness Zone on a regular basis.**

# CHAPTER 6
# EMOTION

Think of emotions as brief experiences of satisfaction or frustration that influence behavior. A view of evolutionary psychology is that emotions evolved to produce the action necessary to survive in a harsh environment. From this perspective, emotions are an appropriate response to negative or positive trigger situations that impact on the survival of our species. We are not aware of the complex mental activity required to continually evaluate the world around us, because instinct operates at an unconscious level. Through the process of comparisonitis and catastrophizing, instinct chugs away in the background and never stops.

Emotions involve a state of arousal of the nervous system with differing conditions and strengths of arousal relating to different emotions. They are extremely potent. Excessive exposure to intense emotion is causally linked to severe and terminal illness. Single experiences of intense emotions have demonstrated the ability to make smart people dumb, to make reasonable people very unreasonable, and to manipulate human behavior. Emotions are powerful stuff, and since our survival instinct throws them at us on a regular basis, it is well worth having a good enough understanding to be able to read them, predict them, normalize them, and utilize them.

By way of example, I am going to focus on three common negative emotions: anxiety, anger, and depression. Most negative emotions are wrongly seen to be roadblocks to satisfaction and happiness. This confusion happens because their normal and essential role in survival is not understood and is at first difficult to grasp. Here is a simple way to understand it all.

Survival prioritizes recognition (R), approval (A), and relative importance (i) over contentment and happiness. So, without you even realizing it, your survival instinct is unconsciously striving for RAi.

**Anxiety.**

When we fail to get what we want, we get frustrated. Instinct turns rising frustration into anxiety, and anxiety agitates us to act. Now that we are motivated, instinct directs our efforts toward lowering frustration and getting RAi. Avoidance is the common response to anxiety, because avoidance initially reduces frustration. And as it happens, avoidance also attracts RAi. We tend to notice when people are avoiding. Avoidance draws attention and recognition. We seek to help them. Individuals who receive help have an increased sense of relative importance. We encourage them. Encouragement provides approval. Avoidance has the potential to decrease frustration and increase RAi. If the satisfaction of avoidance gets high enough, it is even possible to be happy being anxious.

However, the RAi we get from being anxious may not last long enough to accumulate to the level of happiness. In difficult circumstances that can't be changed (like global financial crises and terrorism), everyone is anxious and avoidant. Anxious people aren't very good at giving RAi to others when they themselves are suffering. In situations where your plight is no different from anyone else's, avoidance produces little RAi and little satisfaction. Also, individual differences in instinct's appetite affect how long satisfaction from RAi lasts. Appetite differences in the need for ongoing recognition, approval, and relative importance occur as a result of deprived or diminished RAi in childhood, which has occurred, to some extent, to everyone.

When the half-life of satisfaction is short, and the source of anxiety is constant and difficult to change, frustration levels continue to rise, and society is on its way to the More-on Zone. But instinct's toolbox is far from empty. As frustration continues to accumulate, instinct now employs anger or depression.

### Anger.

Anger is effective at lowering frustration and attracting RAi. In the heat of the moment, the physical action most commonly provoked by anger feeds on and consumes the intense feelings of frustration.

Frustration and anxiety trigger the anger that drives people to take action. Unlike the anxious behavior of avoidance, angry behavior is confrontational and not only outwards at other people, animals, or things. The confrontational behavior can be inwards at oneself, including self-criticism and self-harm. When anger is acted upon, your frustration falls simply because you are doing something. Also, as it happens, when you are angry, others notice. You get recognition fast, because their instinct readily identifies you as a threat.

If your anger is directed at them, you won't get their approval, but you tend to make up for that by giving yourself approval for finally starting to do something about your situation. If your anger is directed at a common threat, they may well give you approval as "the enemy of my enemy is my friend." Anger does result in frustration going down and RAi going up. And, like anxiety, if satisfaction from the RAi gets up high enough, it is even possible to be happy being angry.

### Depression.

Depression is potentially more efficient than either anxiety or anger in lowering frustration and attracting RAi. It reduces frustration with a turbocharged version of avoidance: giving up. It is not too hard to see how instinct could have evolved a "giving up" strategy to survive. In life-and-death situations, action provokes a reaction. When action ceases, the reaction stops. Throughout human history, people have survived by surrendering. They surrendered to be slaves, to be abused, to be miserable. But they survived to fight again another day. Remember that instinct prioritizes survival over comfort, satisfaction, and happiness.

Depression is instinct's last resort to deal with ongoing excessive levels of experienced frustration. As we become increasingly depressed, our motivation and activity levels fall, and our emotions flatten out. The intensity of our feelings disappears. We don't feel much about anything, either positive or negative. Our lowered level of activity means a lower chance of more things going wrong that might cause even more frustration. Providing that the people you are connected with are not too distracted by their own anxiety, they will notice when your interest and motivation drops along with your activity levels. Depression achieves recognition. People will encourage your attempts to do more; this provides approval. People will try to help you as you make an effort to get motivated again, and this provides relative importance. Instinct has learned that depression flattens frustration and attracts RAi. When this happens, satisfaction goes up. But because depression has flattened the intensity of all feelings, there is no chance that satisfaction can ever get high enough for one to be happy while being depressed.

If depression starts to lift (because of many possible reasons), people once again become aware of their underlying frustration. As their frustration levels rise, they again begin to feel anxious. If their anxious behavior does not lower frustration levels, anxiety again becomes anger. Depression is a self-sustaining condition; you are less aware of feeling frustrated at the cost of feeling less of everything, which continues to be dissatisfying and keeps you depressed. Interventions to lift mood and changes in routine to increase activity are necessary to escape the web of depression. When things do start to improve, you have to be ready to deal with an increasing awareness of the frustration and anxiety that the depression had been masking. If you can't get a handle on tolerating the re-emergence of frustration, you will continue to experience cycles of anxiety, anger, and depression throughout your life.

So, there you have it: three negative emotions, all having a valid and significant part to play in your survival. The unpleasantness of sweat keeps your body functioning well. The disturbance of emotion keeps your psychology working well. From your instinct's perspective, you never get emotional unnecessarily. Anxiety and anger are meant to be unpleasant. You will typically procrastinate and avoid doing the things that need to be done when you are anxious. You will usually overreact to things when you are angry in the More-on Zone. You will normally stop reacting to things and stop doing much at all as you get depressed.

The behavior that follows from your having these emotions is necessary for your survival.

I hope that you are seeing by now that the effectiveness of instinctive behavior comes at a high price. It prioritizes survival over quality of life. If you want a bit more happiness in your life, you are going to have to regulate your instinct's interference.

You will need to interpret emotions—yours and others'—a little differently. Emotions are both your fire alarm and your sprinkler system. Your survival instinct has been honed over thousands of years. If it is starving for recognition, approval, or relative importance, your instinct uses anxiety and avoidant behavior to attract more. Anxiety results from the ongoing frustration of a lack of RAi in your life. Anxiety is meant to cause avoidance to attract more RAi. Instinct steps in again with anger when anxiety hasn't been enough to get the recognition, approval, or relative importance it needs. Depression occurs when neither anxiety or anger has been enough to attract the RAi you need. Your depressed feelings and behavior are a last-ditch attempt to increase RAi and deaden your frustration in the meantime.

Emotions are designed to manipulate your behavior and the behavior of those around you in search of recognition, approval, and relative importance. They have to be intense to do so. They can be hard to tolerate at times. If you drug them too much to make them more tolerable, your sprinkler system won't work very well. Eventually, your house is going to burn down.

Although the instinctive behavior produced by emotions efficiently attracts RAi in the short run, the quality of the RAi isn't always that good. Strong emotions can be toxic to others. Reality confronts us with circumstances in which we will normally and naturally begin to feel anxious and become avoidant. You should be feeling anxious, but it is not OK to avoid doing things that are important to others. You will find yourself in situations where it is necessary and healthy to feel angry and act out. But it is not acceptable to threaten or behave aggressively toward others to satisfy your own need for RAi unless you are fighting for your life. Reality also confronts us with situations where it is necessary and normal to feel depressed and give up. But it is important to get out of the ultimate safety and nothingness of depression when other people might be depending on us.

To be happy in spite of yourself, you have to increase your tolerance of emotions, your own and others'. If you remain intolerant of bad feelings, your instinct will continue to dominate your life. Stop assuming that since you are anxious, angry, or depressed that the sky must be falling. You probably don't like to sweat but don't rush to the doctor every time you sweat with a fear of leaking to death. You probably don't want your sweat glands removed. You realize that sweating is necessary for managing body temperature and your health.

Take the "sweat" approach to negative emotions. See them as normal reactions to life situations and the way they impact you as necessary for your survival. Emotions are not necessarily indicative of something wrong with life, with you, with past choices, and your future potential. If you can normalize the way you feel, you can stop catastrophizing about it. If you can do that, you are ready to calm down, work on generating your own RAi, and be able to stick at it until you get the results you want.

Your instinct operates at an unconscious level. You can't hear it, but it can hear you. If you change your experience through changing what you do, you can rewrite your instinct's survival patterns. Reaching an understanding and acceptance of emotion and the operation of the Frustration and Satisfaction Tanks is the path to being happy in spite of yourself.

**Summary.**

- **Instinct seeks recognition, approval, and relative importance for reassurance and safety.**
- **When RAi is lacking, frustration occurs and will eventually trigger anxiety.**
- **Anxiety commonly results in avoidant behavior, which reduces frustration and is rewarded by the RAi it attracts.**
- **Anger uses and burns up frustration and at the same time is rewarded by the RAi it attracts.**
- **Depression is instinct's last resort in seeking safety in a toxic environment. Depression also attracts RAi.**
- **Successfully treating and "lifting" the feeling of depression without being prepared for the subsequent re-emergence of anxiety and anger can make depression a potentially self-sustaining condition.**
- **Realizing that anxiety, anger, and depression are naturally and normally produced by your survival instinct can reduce your catastrophizing about having these feelings.**
- **You can be happy in spite of them.**

# CHAPTER 7
# LIFTING THE FOG OF INSTINCT

Nick is diving under the incoming walls of white water.

He's not sure about surfing today. The swell has been pumping from the southeast for days since the cyclonic low turned out to sea and headed in the direction of New Zealand. The bigger waves out back have got to be over ten feet.

He gets a shock when a body, face down, washes into him in the next wall of white water. He sees a broken leg rope. He can't see the guy's board.

Nick gets lucky. He has just enough time to pull the body onto his board and manages to hang on as the next water wall hits him and washes them into the shore.

He pulls the body up the beach; the guy isn't breathing. He remembers learning cardiopulmonary resuscitation (CPR) as part of qualifying for his bronze lifesaving medallion at Rainbow Bay Surf Club. Nick is shaking as he turns the guy on his side, checks that his tongue and nothing else are blocking his airway, lies him back, and starts CPR.

He remembers that the compressions on the center of the rib cage need to be really strong and rapid, thirty at a time and as fast as two per second. No problem. Nick's instinctive emotional reaction gives him the strength and speed he needs to do this. He remembers that sometimes ribs can break under this pressure, but saving a life makes this a risk worth taking.

CPR is a lifesaving technique taught for emergency use when breathing or the heartbeat has stopped. Although the extreme force required can cause collateral damage, particularly to the young and elderly, CPR might be the only thing that will save someone's life.

Instinct has evolved over thousands of generations to ensure that you and the human species survives and thrives.

- Instinct constantly monitors your exposure to threat or opportunity without you knowing.
- Instinct's database of survival triggers grows along with your life experience.
- Strong feelings control your actions when a survival situation is registered.
- Strong feelings also control your attention, resulting in tunnel vision and repetitive thoughts.
- This control over our actions and our thoughts undermines common sense and happiness; this is the fog of instinct.

At birth, instinct provides a set of survival patterns designed to attract the recognition, approval, and relative importance it needs to ensure survival.

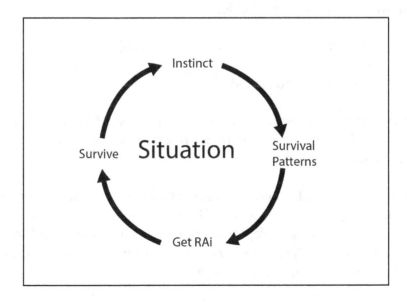

A survival pattern is a blueprint that flags a situation as a threat ("if this happens"); describes the response we should make to the situation ("respond in this way"); and predicts the reaction we can expect from our response ("this will be the result").

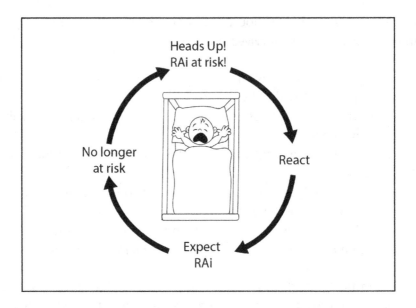

A newborn's pattern might be described as:

- Having pains in the tummy (hunger threat).
- Cry a lot.
- Get noticed and get fed.

Patterns that are present at birth have been hard-wired into our brain by evolution. Some examples of hard-wired patterns relate to hunger, pain, loud noise, and even height.

Patterns not present at birth but learned through repeated exposure to the environment become soft-wired into our brain. These are important; they give us the ability to adapt and survive in a broad range of conditions. The longer we live, the greater our exposure to our environment and the greater the number of acquired survival patterns.

A child's learned survival pattern might be:

- Parents are fighting, violent, unpredictable (threat).
- Keep my head down (don't get noticed).
- I won't get caught up in the trouble.

A teenager's pattern might be:

- My mom is tired (a threat to my RAi).
- Offer to help.
- Will get my RAi from Mom going again.

Or alternatively:

- Mom won't let me go out (a threat to getting RAi from my friends).
- Make her feel guilty about my upset (draw attention to my distress).
- She might let me go.

> **If a child grows up in an environment of erratic or inconsistent reactions from caregivers or influential others, the third element of the survival pattern—"This is what you can expect"—is largely missing or treated as unreliable by instinct. An incomplete or unreliable survival pattern creates significant stress in adult life whenever an experienced situation is similar to an earlier traumatic childhood situation. Children who were unpredictably punished for trying to help will be stressed in their adult relationships when their help is required and may have recurring issues trusting people with whom they are close.**

Instinct compares every new experience with its growing store of survival patterns (what to look for, what to do, and what to expect) looking for matches. If it finds a match, it creates a physical reaction—a feeling. The purpose of this feeling is to manipulate behavior to get enough recognition, approval, and relative importance to survive the new experience. We don't realize we are acting this way, because instinct has created a fog over our conscious awareness. Other people may see that we are attention-seeking—looking for recognition, approval, or importance—but we don't.

We have to lift the fog of instinct.

Having and using an alternative method to generate RAi to create and extend happiness is a key offering of this book. You need to remember and master this method. To help you with this, I want to introduce a second abbreviation.

Most of us know about CPR, and many of us know how to administer it. This procedure already has a memory hook in your conscious mind, including the circumstances of when to use it: life-and-death emergencies.

Just as this physical emergency procedure lists a series of specific actions, the psychological procedure required to lift the fog of instinct denotes a series of specific actions and the order in which they should be done.

> **The purpose of CPR is to restore a physical heartbeat.**
> **The purpose of cPR is to restore a psychological heartbeat (RAi).**

Psychological resuscitation (cPR) is a moderation technique that can be used in threatening situations when comparisonitis and catastrophizing make us and others unhappy. Although cPR might only be able to moderate the extreme power of survival reactions, it can help to achieve the outcome of being alive *and* being happy at least more of the time and for longer periods.

The initial lowercase *c* is important. It not only differentiates this abbreviation from its medical parent, but it also reminds the user of the important first step that is so easy to overlook in the heat of the moment.

- The *c* is for relative calm. When your instinct is triggered by a survival pattern match in your limbic system, the initial physical reaction it causes is intense enough to create a distorted perspective of lost RAi and prompt extreme behavior to replace it. The strength of the initial physical reaction cannot be avoided, but it has to be moderated. The goal of the first step is therefore to moderate the intensity of your initial physical reaction after it has occurred—small c calm.

- *P* is for perspective on your instinct's need for RAi.
- *R* is for restoring RAi back to "instinctively safe" levels.

To be happy in spite of yourself, you need to apply cPR to lift the fog of instinct being caused by comparisonitis and catastrophizing.

### Step 1 of cPR: Calming Frustration.

Your instinct moves from passive scanning to active intervention when the passive scan shows RAi falling to unsafe levels (fear) or shows a massive opportunity to raise RAi to high levels (lust, greed). The fog of instinct begins with active intervention at an unconscious level. Active intervention starts by creating tension, agitation, and irritability to motivate action to restore (or accumulate) RAi. This agitated state turns off your reasonable common sense to allow action to occur without a consideration of the consequences. It does this by shutting out your ability to think ahead.

The first step toward little *c* is to notice your growing irritability, impatience, or agitation. This will happen sooner or later depending on the levels in your Frustration and Satisfaction Tanks. If the intensity of your emotion is high, and if reality is about to end or change your life right then and there, use the intensity of your initial agitation and run, hide, fight, or risk. Do whatever is necessary to survive.

But if your life is not about to end right then and there, you can take steps to calm down a bit if you attribute the cause of your agitation to yourself, to the fog of instinct. Seeing yourself as the cause gives you the power to affect it. Ask yourself: "Just how uptight, edgy, tense, frustrated, anxious, or angry am I?"

It is important to seek at least a rough answer to this question. This draws your attention to the initial intensity of your physical reaction. Later, you can compare your current state of agitation with this initial state to encourage yourself for making progress moving in from the initially high agitation to the little *c* of relative calm. Calm down a little before taking the next step of seeking your instinct's perspective on your current state of RAi.

Any activity that involves physical action works to reduce emotional tension. Movement helps you tolerate and reduce the emotional stress of frustration, because the effort of movement uses the agitation and has the potential to generate a satisfying result at the same time. During movement, you focus on what you are doing, and this dilutes attention to your distress. Action provides relief from emotional tension in the heat of the moment; it has additional benefits in that sustained movement is good in many physical and mental ways for the body. Used as part of your weekly schedule, movement helps to lower the daily level of frustration in your tank and has the potential to increase satisfaction in your tank.

When you first start to use a movement routine, the required effort will be challenging and frustrating. When you have been doing it for a while, attention to the movement and the start-up frustration becomes less noticeable. But it still needs to require enough of your attention so that once you start moving, it gives you relief from past dissatisfaction and current frustration. As you get better at it, you will be able to lose yourself in it. If you don't think of much else while doing the activity, it is working well for you.

You need to have developed some skill in the movement activity before it will be effective in reducing tension in the heat of the moment. The anticipation of doing something physical when we don't have to, or don't want to, can itself be frustrating and hardly satisfying. It can seem illogical to calm down a bit by using an activity that involves start-up frustration. You will need to address this logic if you are going to benefit from the use of movement. You can do this by focusing on the potential value of the activity.

"This is hard today, but so what! It is what it is. It is doing me good. I'm telling myself that I can do it and be a stronger, more confident person because of it."

"Feeling that I don't have time for it today won't stop the satisfaction I get from the activity if I just make the time. Once I get started, I won't focus so much on other stuff that frustrates me, and I know that when I finish, I will think about and handle that other stuff better."

"If I make this a routine, I will impress myself with the ability to do something important and not shy away from it. Non-avoidance will build my confidence in myself. But occasionally I can expect to find it hard to get started and not feel like doing it."

Regular, routine movement will lower the level of frustration in your tank enough to calm down a bit. Lower levels of frustration mean that your overall satisfaction will be less affected by the unhappiness you are yet to deal with.

Distraction is another benefit of activity that diverts your attention away from your current unhappiness. Regular distraction activities lower the daily level of frustration in your tank and help you be relatively calm. The choice and preparation of distraction activities need to be done before distraction can calm you down a bit. There are important considerations regarding the use of distraction, and sorting these out takes logic and common sense, which you won't have access to in the heat of a survival reaction. So, think these issues through before you use distraction to calm down a bit.

Distraction without negative consequences will lower emotional distress. Distraction with negative consequences will also calm you down a bit but will add additional suffering later.

Many distracting activities provide significant immediate relief from emotional distress but have the side effect of increasing dissatisfaction and frustration in the future. Humans find activities that provide immediate relief from emotional distress so highly attractive that we are prone to addiction to these activities, regardless of their future consequences. In this context, addiction refers to the repeated use of activities that cause future problems.

Drugging (alcohol, party drugs, caffeine, nicotine, sugar), spending, gambling, gossiping, complaining, undermining, gaming, over-exercising, over/under-eating are examples of distraction activities that are very popular. They have been around forever, are used by almost everyone, provide rapid temporary satisfaction and relief from frustration, but have the potential to generate dissatisfaction and frustration later.

Doodling, controlled breathing, singing (maybe not aloud), crafting, sporting, gardening, reading, cooking, listening (music, podcasts, counting (not out loud) are examples of distracting activities that provide temporary satisfaction and relief from frustration with the potential to produce future satisfaction and happiness.

In our culture, distracting activities are sold to us as the Holy Grail of happiness. Unfortunately, the ones with adverse side effects are the most popular, because they are the quickest and most reliable in providing immediate satisfaction and relief from frustration. Their widespread availability and popularity make them easily accessible, and they create fortunes for those who sell them to us. It is these not-so-good ones that have the potential to generate the most collateral damage and unhappiness in life.

But it is what it is. We aren't going to stop the use of distraction in the search for frustration relief, satisfaction, and happiness just because someone says that although distraction does work in the short run, it is not good for us over the long term.

We will keep using these activities because distraction works. They do provide rapid satisfaction and relief from frustration, even if only temporarily. What you can do to use these diversions efficiently is to think more about the future frustration and dissatisfaction associated with their use and act accordingly.

Don't overuse pure distraction activities; they are potentially addictive. Mix up the ones you do use so that you don't overuse any one. Keep in mind that stepping away from the current frustration of your unhappy situation is a relief for you but can add to future dissatisfaction and the frustration and resentment of others around you. You don't want that to happen too much if their resentment impacts your satisfaction and frustration.

When you are using distraction activities, there is a fine line between self-interest behavior (moderating your frustration and satisfaction) and selfish behavior (creating more frustration and dissatisfaction for others in the process).

Examples:

"I know stewing is normal, but occasionally I need a break from it, especially when I am just going around and around in circles. I can try gardening or cooking or reading or a glass of wine to help me focus on something else for a while. Then I can come back to supporting my instinct by making room for stewing. Stewing will stop when I come up with a formula for RAi. It is what it is."

"If I find that uninvited negative thoughts pop into my head and interrupt my focus or peace of mind, I can decide whether to pay attention to these ideas. If I choose not to, I can use counting backwards (in words from a three-digit number—six hundred and seventy-two, six hundred and seventy-one, six hundred and seventy... It doesn't take many numbers to move stewing thoughts into the background). Providing I count inside my head, and my lips aren't moving, I can continue to pay attention to my current activity while the counting keeps my stewing in the background where it will have much less impact on me. I can't and don't want to stop uninvited thoughts from popping into my head. I need a new formula for RAi. I just want my stewing to be more in the background."

Instead of counting, you could use singing (inside your head or out loud depending on where you are), doodling, fiddling, tapping, humming, or whistling.

Drugging your instinct also effectively changes the impact of uninvited thoughts by depressing or stimulating brain function. But the distortion to brain function caused by drugging affects not only your survival strategies; drugging distorts all the activity between your ears. Drugging interrupts comparisonitis and initially minimizes catastrophizing. But it also changes mental processes like reaction time, logic, tolerance, and the persistence you need to better manage the frustrating and dissatisfying circumstances with which you are dealing. Sometimes drugging does lead to satisfying outcomes without collateral damage. When this occurs, it mostly only happens when the extent of drugging distortion is small. So, it is important to regulate the use of drugging. You need to minimize the extent of the sensory distortion that drugging causes.

More often, however, even minimal distortion interferes with your attempts to regulate your use of whatever drug you are using. And if the potency of the drug you are using is unknown, or you lack experience with regulating its effects, you can't control its use entirely. In these cases, the brief relief and satisfaction caused by drug use will be followed by significant dissatisfaction and frustration. Dissatisfaction will occur as your increasing sensory distortion has an increasingly negative effect on your behavior, and you get kickback from the circumstances you are dealing with.

While careful regulation can minimize the potential collateral damage of drugging, we humans don't have a good track record of careful use.

"When I am worried about having to deal with my circumstances (stewing), I usually eat (sugar and carbohydrates) or drink (alcohol) or use other drugs or spend too much. The brief satisfaction I get from these activities can push my uninvited thoughts into the background but always leaves me feeling dissatisfied with myself afterwards. Next time I find myself stewing (thinking unwanted thoughts), I am going to tell myself that these thoughts are normal. At the same time, I will have a couple of different distraction activities ready to go. I expect any of these activities to take longer and work a little less well than drugging or spending, but the effort might be worthwhile, and I might enjoy seeing myself as a stronger person."

**Step 2 of cPR: Perspective on RAi.**

Now that you are into small c mode, you are ready to make conscious the comparisonitis and catastrophizing that create your instinct's sensitivity to having lost RAi.

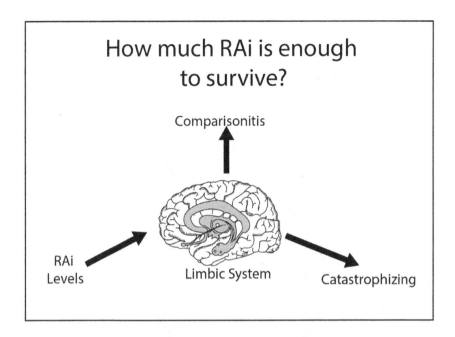

Instinct automatically decides how much RAi is necessary for safety and security. Since the goal of survival requires erring on the side of caution (better to be safe than sorry), comparisonitis is mostly negative, and subsequent catastrophizing increases the intensity of any physical reaction. Left to its own devices, instinct almost always sees the worst and catastrophizes about insufficient RAi. Once a survival pattern is triggered, instinct makes you further frustrated, dissatisfied, and insecure. These feelings have evolved to drive you into survival reactions to restore RAi without any consideration of the collateral damage of these reactions to the RAi of others or of the future impact on you of this collateral damage. Instinct makes smart people do dumb things.

Instinct has learned through experience that anxiety, anger, and depression are all strong motivators. Instinct uses these negative emotions to drive reactions that generate RAi.

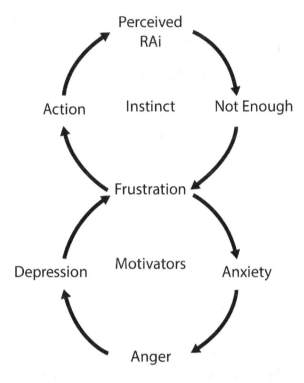

To minimize the likelihood of survival reactions from our instinct creating collateral damage on others, we need to take personal responsibility for restoring RAi and stop putting the responsibility for our RAi on others. Our instinct is influenced by and can learn from what we do. It can benefit from our conscious efforts to restore RAi.

When you find your thoughts refusing to move on from an event, you are experiencing stewing, a symptom of comparisonitis and catastrophizing. The general form of stewing thoughts look like:

- *It shouldn't have happened that way. That is not acknowledging me, approving of me, or considering my importance.*
- *It should have happened this way to respect me, value me, and recognize my importance.*
- *I should have prevented it to get recognition, approval, and to demonstrate my importance.*
- *I should have responded to it in a way to ensure my recognition, approval, and importance.*

- *I should have, could have, would have acted differently if I was recognized, if I was not afraid of disapproval, if I was important enough.*
- *It is so unfair, it's not my fault, I don't deserve this.*
- *It's their fault, they deserve …*

At first you will have to guess to find the detail in these ideas. These details are hidden in the unconscious part of your mind. However, once you start consciously looking for them, you will begin to identify with them. If you look at stewing as the work of instinct grieving for lost RAi, stewing provides you with clues to the information you need to reach an understanding of your state of RAi. The "shoulds" and the "should-nots"; the "unfairs" and the "awfuls"; the "unbearables" and the criticisms of yourself and others provide the clues to your instinct's RAi sensitivity. Stewing goes on and on and on until you get it—until you reach a perspective about your missing RAi and decide to do something about restoring it.

---

### Micromanaging

**In an attempt to gain more recognition, approval, and relative importance from looking at past situations differently, or from planning the perfect response in a future situation, a common and unhelpful focus is to look at how you might change the perspective and behavior of others. However, it is next to impossible to come up with a plan that will consistently attract RAi from others. The difficulty of manipulating or coercing them to give you RAi with any consistency lies in the 84,000 variables affecting their lives that are outside of your influence. These external variables can readily nullify your efforts to influence them, especially when you and your influence is not around, and their instinct takes over when it feels under threat.**

---

The following examples of how to modify stewing to create RAi can be used as self-talk templates to create a perspective on recognition, approval, and relative importance. Instinct's perspective is that RAi comes from the outside. Self-talk modifies this perspective to produce RAi from the inside, providing you guide your self-talk with a perspective on your own needs.

Two sources of RAi (external and internal) are better than one for survival and happiness.

"I don't like myself when I am stewing. I get frustrated with mental fatigue, physical tiredness, going around and round and not seeming to be getting anywhere, not being able to sleep, being so distracted by stewing as to be unable to concentrate on the task at hand, making mistakes, forgetfulness. But I know my stewing can help me find ways to increase RAi."

Stewing is an automatic process your instinct uses to generate RAi. The negative side effects of stewing include feelings of frustration, of inadequacy, of being victimized, of rejection, of being insignificant. To minimize these side effects and tolerate stewing without it actually undermining your RAi, you need to put up an "Instinct at Work" sign. This sign can help normalize stewing as a natural and helpful process.

"It is natural for me to be distressed by stewing. I will catastrophize about it and want to stop doing it. However, my instinct needs to stew to formulate a perspective on my missing RAi. This perspective will help me restore RAi tomorrow and is worth the distress of stewing today."

"My anger at myself when I can't stop stewing is caused by instinct's fear of weakness and running out of RAi. It is natural for me to criticize myself about my inability to control my thoughts. It is also necessary to keep stewing until my instinct is clear about the RAi I need to restore. Stewing is like sweating; it is uncomfortable but only happens when it needs to. Stewing is evidence of my instinct at work."

"If I dislike myself for the natural and instinctive responses I have when stewing, I will only further undermine my RAi."

"I don't like the bad feeling I get when I am stewing, but a distressing feeling won't harm me, and it is entirely reasonable to feel this way. Distress is an ordinary and necessary side effect of stewing over past frustration and dissatisfaction. I can take steps to better tolerate the suffering of stewing so I can get clarity on my RAi needs."

"Instinct uses stewing to plan and survive. It is what it is. Stewing has no bearing on my competency or my strength of character. I only stew when I need to. I am ready for instinct's catastrophizing about weakness and expect to stew today so I can be clear about what I want tomorrow."

These thoughts are examples of what is happening first at an unconscious level in the limbic system and then at a conscious level in the frontal lobe. They are examples of moderating instinctive survival responses to situations that may not be survival situations.

The purpose of perspective is to normalize the inability to stop thinking about frustration and dissatisfaction and to accept stewing as a necessary side effect of searching for RAi. Perspective deliberately looks for acceptance that "it is what it is," and then to the commitment of thoughts and action that might be useful in tolerating and then restoring lost RAi.

"Stewing is healthy; I should expect to stew."

The actions and outcomes referred to above as examples of perspective self-talk only need to be possible. The goal of perspective is to accept the distress of stewing and to highlight its usefulness. Usefulness of any activity is defined as acting in a way that will increase RAi, lower frustration, and increase satisfaction. You are not trying to come up with a perspective that guarantees lower frustration or higher satisfaction; your perspective just needs to offer the possibility.

So, what do you do with the perspective of Step 2?

- Focus on generating RAi from self-talk before you concentrate on manipulating others to give you RAi.
- Reduce catastrophizing and increase your acceptance of the distress of stewing by using perspective to create an "Instinct at Work" sign.
- Use a perspective on recognition, approval, and relative importance to highlight your situational needs for RAi.
- With such a perspective, you are ready for restoration.

**Step 3 of cPR: Restoration of RAi**

Perspective on missing RAi will normalize instinct's catastrophizing and prepare you for the goal of restoration. Restoration of satisfaction when faced with repetitive stewing requires you to:

- Restore recognition.
- Restore approval.
- Restore importance.

Restoration requires:

- An openness for action.
- A willingness to take risks.
- A determination to learn from outcomes.
- An ability to improvise and adapt.

Dealing with unwanted circumstances can lead to such intense levels of frustration that you readily get to the point of giving up. If you get stopped by your bad feelings, you can get moving again by following the restoration routine of risk-taking and action learning.

Effective risk-taking requires you to:

- Assess the possible consequences of your actions before you take them.
- Put a value on the worthiness of the risk.
- Work up the courage to take the risk.
- Have in place strategies to tolerate the anxiety associated with the proposed risk.

A method of measuring the value of a risk is to estimate the balance between the anxiety of taking the risk (the downside) and the future satisfaction from taking the risk (the upside). If you are likely to be satisfied with the future consequences of your action, and you can tolerate the frustration, it's worth taking. If you are likely to be dissatisfied with future consequences, then it's not worth taking. Even if you are satisfied now, you need to think about future satisfaction. Satisfaction today is not worth dissatisfaction tomorrow.

You don't require a crystal ball to evaluate risks. All you need do is take some time and think about possible future consequences. Action learning requires a definition of success and a means of objective measurement of progress. It requires a focus on acquiring the skills needed for development, the motivation to practice these skills, and the openness to keep adapting efforts in the face of objective evidence.

The restoration ideas and strategies that you plan and put into action only need a possibility of success. You are not going to come up with a plan that guarantees minimum frustration, satisfaction, confidence, and happiness, because 84,000 things in your environment will continue to affect the outcome. This means that no matter how carefully you plan for an outcome, something may still go wrong.

An important element of restoration is to include self-talk that motivates intent and planning strategies to tolerate the anxiety of taking action (little *c*).

To be happy in spite of yourself requires an understanding of:

- Instinct.
- Emotion.
- RAi.
- cPR.

This understanding provides the framework to manage the variables that influence your experience of happiness. In the second part of this book, you will see many examples of how to use this framework in different life contexts, including:

- Relationships, socializing, and breaking up.
- Parenting.
- Working and competition.
- Bureaucracy.
- Retirement, aging, and chronic pain.

These examples illustrate the strategy for being happy in specific situations despite the unwanted interference of instinct on your mood and behavior. All of these examples are drawn from my 40 years of casework as a clinical psychologist. Read as many as are interesting or relevant to you keeping in mind that mastery requires habits and habits are developed through repetition.

**Summary.**

- **When instinct is triggered, it controls our behavior and creates a fog over our common sense.**
- **Instinct seeks survival by demanding recognition, approval, and relative importance from others.**
- **Instinct's power comes from stressful feelings that ensure survival but creates collateral damage to our own and others' contentment and happiness.**
- **To be both safe and happy we need an additional source of RAi.**
- **We can create our own RAi with cPR—a little calm, perspective, and restoration.**
- **cPR combines distraction with self-talk, action, and adaptation.**

# CHAPTER 8
# RELATIONSHIPS

Emily recognized Nick right away. She remembered him from high school as the popular kid with all the sporting awards. She didn't know him that well, and he wasn't in her academic class, but she had wondered what had become of him when he dropped out toward the end of year 11.

Emily had completed school and gone on to college. That was five years ago. Nick didn't seem to have changed much in that time—maybe filled out a bit. He was still the center of attention as he joked with the group he was in. Emily was surprisingly pleased she had decided to come tonight. She really wasn't the party type, but her best friend Jessica was always telling her she had to get a life outside of her work, which was all very easy for Jessica to say. Jessica was the girl that got attention wherever she went. She was drop-dead gorgeous.

Nick noticed Jessica almost the instant she entered the room. She was stunning. But then he recognized Emily. He'd had a crush on her in high school. Emily was the quiet, studious type, so different from the girls in the group that he hung with. He wasn't sure why he'd had a crush on her then, but whatever it was, it was still happening. Yet it didn't matter, as she never seemed to notice him at school and was unlikely to recognize him now.

Neither one of them expected to be recognized by the other. However, a little while later, their eyes met in the crowded room, and they smiled. Massive amounts of RAi went back and forth over that evening as they caught up with each other. They were married less than a year later.

Relationships form when there is a mutual exchange of RAi. When intimate relationships occur, part of the RAi can be instinctive, physical attraction. We can't really explain why we get turned on; we just do. The best non-scientific explanation we can come up is calling it "chemistry." It is either there or it isn't. It's on or off. It's instinct.

Relationships last while RAi lasts. Relationships sour and end when the mutual exchange of RAi breaks down. This breakdown of RAi happens all too easily because:

- The type of recognition, approval, and importance that individuals seek continues to change as they are affected by their accumulating life experience.
- Being distracted by their own challenges in adapting to their life experience, individuals readily miss and consequently don't respond to their partner's changing needs for RAi.
- The impact of exchanged RAi weakens when the novelty begins to wear off.
- High ongoing need for RAi created in individuals by their negative childhood experience exhausts their partner's ability to inject RAi into the relationship.
- High need for RAi makes individuals vulnerable to sources of RAi outside of the relationship. These external sources are highly rewarding for the individual's RAi and toxic to their partner's RAi.

These situations first impact relationships at a mostly unconscious level. Insight into the real cause of negative feelings is almost universally absent.

Typical explanations attribute unhappiness to circumstances (star signs, alignment of the planets, and phases of the moon) and the behavior of others—partners, family, friends, and children.

"I have outgrown him. I just don't love him anymore."

"She is too hard to live with, and her kids don't like me."

"He has treated me so badly over the years. He has never really supported me."

"The moment we got together she started trying to change me."

"Her family has never accepted me."

"I knew he was screwing around behind my back. I was just not willing to face it. My kids need a roof and a father."

"I don't know how it happened. The guy I met at work cared more for me than my partner did."

"My youngest child moved out, and I had no more reason to stay."

Regarding these explanations, circumstances may or may not have happened the way they are described. Whether something actually happened the way you see it is not important. What matters is the way you think it happened. Beauty is in the eye of the beholder and so is fact, truth, and reality. You can work on your happiness when you have exposed your neediness for RAi and then change how you go about addressing this need. You are going to be a lot less dependent on the universe to recognize you, approve of you, and deem you important. You don't have to wait to be discovered by anyone to be happy more often and for longer.

Intimate relationships (physical, emotional, spiritual) have the potential to be closer, more personal, and more meaningful than general socializing. We find ourselves feeling, thinking, and acting differently than we would in a less personal relationship. The comments, conclusions, and examples in this chapter are useful and relevant to a range of one-on-one relationships, including friendships, sibling relationships, mentoring relationships, and the full spectrum of mating and dating relationships— any one-on-one relationship that is important to you.

Socializing: With social media, it has become easier to find groups that are accepting and validating. But this convenience has a significant downside. First, it has greatly increased the potential for being exposed to the toxic behavior of other group members (disapproval, rejection, cyber bullying). Secondly, the ease of turning on your phone or computer encourages the development of a time-consuming obsession to regularly check on approval and rejection ratings and an urgency and capability to take action to protect relative importance (via texting, Twitter, Facebook, and many other avenues).

How often do you see people out together who are attending more to their phones than to each other? Social media requires less effort than face-to-face socializing and is beginning to dominate our social behavior. But because of the compulsive nature of cyber socializing, less effort is not equating to less time and more RAi. The increased exposure of cyber socializing subjects us to less satisfaction and more frustration, as our comparisonitis pays more attention to potential disapproval and rejection than to approval and acceptance.

Once the digital posts start flying back and forth in your group, you feel pressure to contribute. Otherwise, how will you maintain RAi in the group? When you do contribute, does your comment get as much response as someone else's? Maybe your post gets no response at all. This is anxiety-provoking stuff for your instinct.

Socializing is an instinctive drive necessary for your sense of safety, but the ease of cyber socializing exposes you to large numbers of people who, like you, are looking for a sense of security and safety through notice and approval. When everyone's instinct is calling, "look at me, respond to me, approve of me," not everyone can get the attention their instinct wants.

**Objectively measuring progress in getting more out of socializing could be identifying what kind of RAi you look for in social situations. Look for moments where you feel good about yourself. These occasions could be when you remember the names of others in your group, talking one-on-one when in a group, openly asking more about the topic being discussed by others, or contributing your viewpoint about a subject. If you can't specify any particular moments, this is an opportunity for risk-taking. Put yourself out there and follow up on that action that you have been putting off for ages. You know what it is. Get anxious, tolerate your anxiety, do it anyway, and explore your ability to generate your own RAi in spite of how on edge you might feel at the time.**

**Objectively measuring progress in socializing might be recording the number of times that you put yourself in social situations each week, looking to see a gradual increase in frequency. You could keep a record of the number of times you volunteer your point of view; or the number of times you put forward suggestions about what to do, say, or think; or the number of invites you make. Objective measurement requires clear evidence of progress. That's where the number of times comes in.**

**"Making an effort to tolerate my discomfort when I socialize, to accept the way it is, and to come up with a plan of action to continue in spite of it is frustrating, and I can't be sure if it will be worth it. But I am confident that instinct needs to socialize to maintain a source of recognition, approval, and relative importance to ensure my survival."}**

Instinct has a survival plan based on the belief that there is security in a group and safety in numbers. In an intimate relationship, the group size is two, not large enough for safety. Nevertheless, the reason intimate relationships are unique to our survival is that instinct has learned that the inherent high quality of RAi in this special group can be more important that numbers.

Because instinct puts quality of RAi before numbers, it places lots of emphasis and high expectations on the quality remaining unchanged over time. Once the initial euphoria of an intimate relationship wears off, comparisonitis works overtime looking to reassure instinct that RAi is not changing. But comparisonitis has a negative bent, and so it pays more attention to negative change than to positive change.

The reality that RAi drops as time goes on is a natural and normal instinctive reaction in intimate relationships. Fluctuations in quality in an intimate relationship are inevitable. No two people can remain in a relationship bubble where nothing else matters for very long. Eventually, one or the other will be impacted by an outside event that pulls their attention far enough away from the relationship for their disconnection to be noticed by the other. When this happens, unconscious comparisonitis creates feelings of neglect or unimportance that generate conscious thoughts of being disregarded, devalued, or taken for granted. These thoughts lead to words of accusation or actions to *test* the other's commitment. The words are typically responded to with defensiveness or denial. This test is frequently failed because of the distraction caused by the outside event. Blame then leads to counter-blame. Frustration increases, and RAi falls.

The expectations and constantly high standards of relationship quality in intimate relationships make ongoing satisfaction and happiness exceptionally challenging—perhaps more challenging than in any other relationship. It is a paradox that the relationship that has the potential to offer the most happiness in our lives can produce the greatest amount of unhappiness.

**Rubber Meets the Road.**

To increase your confidence and satisfaction in intimate relationships:

- Start by getting clear about what you want from your relationship. What made it special at first? What were you expecting from it? How do you want it to be now? How do you want it to be in the future? Answers to these questions may be different depending on whether you are thinking about yourself or your partner.

- Look for the unconscious "shoulds" and "should nots" that are currently creating your frustration and undermining your RAi.
- Reality test and replace these thoughts with a perspective and a strategy that allows you to get what you want (less frustration) and restore your RAi (more satisfaction).

Frustration and diminished RAi only occur when things are not the way they should be. So, ask yourself:

- What are my frustrations in my relationship? Look for the "shoulds" or "should nots" creating your frustration when things don't happen the way they should.
- What are the "shoulds" or "should nots" that determine my recognition, approval, and importance in my relationships?

**As a rule, try not to "should" on yourself or anyone else. The fewer the number of "shoulds" (or "should nots") in your life, the better for you and for others.**

. . .

Nick is struggling. After he dropped out of school and surfed for the next year and a half living on handouts from his mom and income from the occasional laboring job, he realized that he had to do more to get more out of his life. The plumber he was laboring for recognized him to be a good worker and showed his approval by offering Nick an apprenticeship. Nick was stoked. He felt important, and he made sure he didn't let his boss down. He excelled in his apprenticeship.

Now he is a boss himself. He is working as a subcontractor on a huge building site and has employed two plumbers and an apprentice to help him. He is feeling responsible for them and their families' security as well as the security of Emily and his two kids Jake and Abbey.

The giant building company he is working for is behind on paying him for the plumbing work he has done. They keep talking about a global financial crisis. He can't stop working for them; they owe him too much. He has to continue on the job hoping that they will come good with a payment. Meanwhile, his material costs are increasing, and wages have to be paid. He thinks he is letting everyone down. He should be able to handle this. He shouldn't have taken this job. He should have known he was growing his business too quickly. He shouldn't have been so damn greedy and let his success go to his head. He is thinking he is not the man that Emily married—the man he should be. He has let his kids down. He should have thought ahead more.

The home that he and Emily built after Emily became pregnant is collateral for his plumbing business and is now under threat. He has used all his overdraft. The bank that was eager to loan him money two years ago is now treating him like a number, not like a person. It should treat him better, but in a global financial crisis, it doesn't care about him. He keeps telling Emily everything is OK, but that light at the end of the tunnel has almost gone out for Nick. All he can think to do is work harder, and he is getting exhausted. It is looking like the bank is going to force him to sell their house. How is he going to tell Emily that?

Emily is always tired. Jake is four years old, and Abbey is still in her "terrible twos." She can't remember when she slept through the night. Nick is so distant. She knows that money has been tight recently and has asked him if everything is OK. Nick is working for one of the biggest building companies on the coast, and she believes his work is going well. So why is he so distant? Her intuition tells her something is wrong; he should tell her.

Emily thinks she has found the answer in the mirror. She can't see the vibrant girl that got Nick's attention that night of the party despite the allure of Jessica. Two kids, constant tiredness: How does anyone remain attractive under these conditions? She should take care of herself better. She is letting herself down and is angry with herself for being so weak.

If Nick was willing to help out a bit more and would get up at night more often as he should—or come home early occasionally and cook dinner like he used to do—she could pay a little more attention to herself, get back to her jogging, her fitness, her attractiveness, and her libido.

Speaking of libido, she can't remember the last time he "wanted" her. This is all so different from what she expected from marriage. She thought she had found a good man and had a good relationship. It shouldn't be like this.

From Emily's perspective, Nick is taking her for granted, he's expecting too much from her, and he isn't doing enough to support her. Her kids need her, but Nick obviously doesn't. She has found a side of Nick that she doesn't like.

Many of us have thought about giving up an on intimate relationships because it was too hard. However, at an instinctive level, we will continue seeking the ideal one-on-one relationship. The feeling of being in love, of being loved, and the intense approval in such a relationship is deemed by instinct to ensure the survival of our species. One love is worth more than any number of likes.

Remember the Chicken Little story? When things happen in an intimate relationship that your instinct deems to be falling acorns, you will experience increasingly negative physical reactions which promote unconscious and then conscious catastrophizing. Unless you find your "shoulds" and intervene, your instinct can lead to the very outcomes that you may not initially want—in this case the ending of a relationship.

**Psychological Resuscitation.**

**Step 1 of cPR: Calming Frustration.**

While the perspective and restoration required to resuscitate happiness will be different from situation to situation, achieving small $c$, a little bit of calm, is the first and necessary step regardless of the situation. Movement and distraction are great activities for attaining small $c$; see Chapter 7 for details on getting small $c$ and to remind yourself of the risks of drug use.

**Step 2 of cPR: Perspective on RAi.**

Emily can search the three dimensions of RAi to better understand the distressing perspective of her current circumstances and her marriage. She needs to ask questions of herself.

The first question is about being noticed:

- *Am I sensitive about my recognition in my relationship?* (Observe the comparisonitis in her thoughts.)

"Nick is acting distant (and he shouldn't be). He seems to have no real interest in me and the kids (and he should). He used to help more. He should be helping me more. This is so unfair. I deserve a break. My job is twenty-four hours a day. He isn't helping me out, and he isn't putting in the way he used to. He isn't even trying. If he cared about me, he would notice my tiredness and know that I need a break. It's clear I am not important to him. I thought he loved me."

The second question is about approval:

- *Am I sensitive about the approval I am getting in my relationship?*

"I know I give Nick a tough time every now and again. I just get so tired, and he is always working overtime and is never here. Sometimes I think he likes his job more than he likes me. I know I yell at the kids every now and again, and I feel so bad about that. Maybe I am a bad mother; maybe that's what Nick thinks about me."

The third question is about importance:

- *Am I sensitive about no longer being important to Nick, about no longer being important to anyone?* (The comparisonitis is again clear in her thoughts.)

"Nick used to come home early from work occasionally, and we would go down and eat fish and chips on the beach for dinner. Now he always comes home late (and he shouldn't). Even when he gets home, I can see that his thoughts are somewhere else. Is there someone else? That would explain why I am no longer important to him. Before kids, I was doing important work in my job. Now I am so tired I am barely managing just being a mother. What has happened to me?"

You must first bring these thoughts to the surface before you can moderate the collateral damage that they cause.

**"To learn the secrets of life, we must first become aware of them." (Albert Einstein)**

Below are examples of surfaced thoughts that, once identified, can be normalized to moderate instinct's sensitivity to perceived loss of RAi in relationships.

HMS Unconscious Thoughts

Relationships

You may identify with some of them. You don't need to find all of your instinct's comparisonitis and catastrophizing. All you need to do is to identify a small number of clear thoughts that highlight instinct's fears. The work we do with a few will generalize to all of them and prepare us to move on to restoration.

Examples:

"My goal as a partner (friend, sibling, child, or parent) is to maintain the 'specialness' and satisfaction in my relationship over time by loving my partner and hoping that I will be loved in return. I believe that the way to achieve this outcome is to focus more on noticing, validating, and tolerating my partner rather than on whether they are noticing, validating, and tolerating me."

"I know my instinct seeks validation to feel safe and secure. I also understand that this can't happen all of the time because events outside my relationship will impact my partner and take their attention away from me. When this happens as it eventually must, the sky is not falling; this is only an acorn. This is when I need to love myself."

---

**The concept of love as a feeling is confusing to most people.**

**"I still love my partner, but I am not 'in love' with him."**

***What does that mean?***

**"I don't know. I have just fallen out of love."**

**Love is commonly credited with almost mythical powers. "Love makes the world go around"; "Love protects us from evil"; "Hate cannot drive out hate. Only love can do that." In the dating/ mating game, "love" is a scary word to say to your partner. Give the typical guy a choice between going to the dentist and discussing love, and he will choose the dentist every time.**

**A way to reach a simple understanding of love and its powers that even men can understand is to refer to love as an *action* word instead of a *feeling* word. When you love someone, something, or yourself, you act in a certain way. Love as an action is discussed in the next section on restoration.**

---

"Reassuring my instinct is important. Deliberately focusing on what I can control—namely acting in ways to notice, value, and tolerate my partner—is the way to the exchange of RAi that will reassure my instinct. If it is to be, then it's up to me. I know I will fail to do this some of the time and start demanding validation and reassurance. Demanding it isn't useful and just adds blame to the current negativity in my relationship. Once I realize I am doing this, I need to satisfy myself. If it is to be, then it is up to me—not my partner."

"If the worst did happen, and my relationship failed, the sky has not fallen. I have the ability to survive."

"My relationship is important and will impact my RAi. That is a good reason to get wound up about it. Getting wound up is like sweating: It only happens when it needs to."

"I understand that my instinct sees approval as important for survival. It pushes me to seek the attention and approval of other people to raise my relative importance. Its fear of rejection winds me up when I am worrying. It believes that I have to be special to be safe, and if I am not special, I risk rejection. This is the way instinct has learned to survive. This is the way it should be. I can react to this reality by topping up my own RAi when I am not getting enough of it from others."

"For my survival instinct, not showing enough interest in me means my partner is not attracted to me. If my value has dropped, it can no longer feel safe, and my instinct wants to blame my partner for that. So, I can expect to feel anxious and angry."

"If my partner puts themselves before me, it must mean that I am no longer important. It shouldn't be that way. I am supposed to be the most important thing in my partner's life. If I can't change this back to the way it used to be, I have to get out. And, anyway, why should it be me that makes all the effort? If my partner won't do it on their accord, that means they don't care enough."

"According to my instinct, my partner wouldn't treat their family or friends the way they treat me, which means I am no longer important. If

I can't make myself valuable, I cannot be safe in this relationship. Instinct is good at catastrophizing, it is hard not to be affected by it. But I can test the reality of my instinct's fears if I calm down a bit. I can also love myself."

These ideas are examples of what is happening first at an unconscious level in the limbic system, and then at a conscious level in the frontal lobes. They illustrate survival responses in situations that are not survival situations. In almost all circumstances, the success or failure of a relationship is not a life-and-death situation.

"Instinct is criticizing me for continuing to allow my partner to take advantage of me and for losing my independence in the eyes of other people outside of my relationship. I understand that if instinct sees me as becoming weak, I am therefore much more vulnerable to the threat of imminent death. Instinct is good at catastrophizing. No wonder I feel so hurt, insecure, and angry."

If it was pointed out to her, Emily is more than capable of understanding:

- How the RAi in her relationship is being blocked by her reactive "shoulds" to circumstances outside of the relationship.
- How these circumstances are serious but not of life-and-death significance, and they do not warrant "shoulds."
- How her instinct is relating to these circumstances as if they are life-and-death and consequently accelerating her loss of RAi by accelerating comparisonitis and catastrophizing.

But this understanding will elude her and Nick (he is "shoulding" on himself something fierce) while they remain exhausted, angry, and fearful. Sometimes briefly stepping away from problems when they seem the worst can produce enough relief from frustration, enough little *c*, to be able to deal with it all differently. The kids could spend a few days with their grandparents; Emily and Nick could get away together, get some sleep, and re-discover the RAi that is still there in their relationship.

**Step 3 of cPR: Restoration of RAi.**

Perspective on missing RAi will normalize Emily's catastrophizing and prepare her for the goal of restoration. To restore satisfaction and happiness when faced with relationship difficulties requires you to:

- Restore recognition.
- Restore approval.
- Restore importance.

Restoration requires:

- An openness for action.
- A willingness to take risks.
- A determination to learn from outcomes.
- An ability to improvise and adapt.

Dealing with unwanted circumstances can lead to such intense levels of frustration that you readily get to the point of giving up. If you get stopped by your bad feelings, you can get moving again by following the restoration routine of risk-taking and action learning.

Effective risk-taking requires you to:

- Assess the possible consequences of your actions before you take them.
- Put a value on the worthiness of the risk.
- Work up the courage to take the risk.
- Have in place strategies to tolerate the anxiety associated with the proposed risk.

A method of measuring the value of a risk is to estimate the balance between the anxiety of taking the risk (the downside) and the future satisfaction from taking the risk (the upside). If you are likely to be satisfied with the future consequences of your action, and you can tolerate the frustration, it's worth taking. If you are likely to be dissatisfied with future consequences, then it's not worth taking. Even if you are satisfied now, you need to think about future satisfaction. Satisfaction today is not worth dissatisfaction tomorrow.

You don't require a crystal ball to evaluate risks. All you need do is take some time and think about possible future consequences. Action learning requires a definition of success and a means of objective measurement of progress. It requires a focus on acquiring the skills needed for development, the motivation to practice these skills, and the openness to keep adapting efforts in the face of objective evidence.

The restoration ideas and strategies that you plan and put into action only need a possibility of success. You are not going to come up with a plan that guarantees minimum frustration, satisfaction, confidence, and happiness, because 84,000 things in your environment will continue to affect the outcome. This means that no matter how carefully you plan for an outcome, something may still go wrong.

**LOVE is the default restoration strategy.**

As an example, one course of action to evaluate and restore RAi revolves around the idea of love. If you think of love as something you do rather than something you feel, the word "love" can be used as an acronym to provide a guide for resuscitation. The acronym of LOVE will move you through a course of action that will enrich the RAi in your relationship.

**L**—stands for listening in an active way. Active listening requires you to hear your partner and then reflect what you think your partner means. The risk here is that your partner might say you don't get it, are wrong, don't care enough to be right, and so on. (If that happens, you try again, listen some more, and then reflect some more.) The value of active listening is that when acknowledged as being accurate, it boosts your partner's sense of relative importance. Your partner's instinct concludes that you care enough and listen enough to get it right.

Most of us rarely employ active listening because it takes too long, or because there are too many opportunities to get it wrong in the eyes of your partner, and it is just easier to say OK. We all value being listened to in an active way. It rarely happens.

**O**—stands for overlooking. Reducing the disapproval that you show your partner over the things they do that trigger your survival instinct can significantly improve their sense of your acceptance and approval. To do this, you need to consciously remind yourself that things are mostly not life-and-death. This reality test helps you tolerate instinct's conclusion that your partner's continued doing of things that bug you means you are unimportant. The extreme example of overlook is "If you can't say anything good, don't say anything at all." A more moderate version of overlooking is to significantly reduce the number of things in your relationship that you are not willing to overlook.

**V**—stands for valuing. When you do things that your partner approves of—things that are important to your partner—your partner feels valued. Relative importance is nurtured and maintained. Once you realize that what is important to your partner changes over time, you are in the position to consistently value your partner and preserve their relative importance. To adequately appreciate your partner, you need to listen and observe with active reflection. If you do this, the things you do for or with your partner and the opportunities you create for your partner will remain consistent with their changing perspective on life. You will keep up to date.

**E**—stands for effort, consistency of effort. If you love your garden, you will water it, and it will thrive. However, if you water it once a month or once a year, it most likely won't flourish (unless it can get water from somewhere else). When effort in a relationship is inconsistent, this is what often happens. Your partner gets "water"—a sense of relative importance—from somewhere else. You nurture relative importance in your relationship with the actions of love and making time for regular loving.

Once a course of action has been set, effective risk-taking requires an assessment of the possible consequences of your actions before you execute them; valuing the worthiness of the risk; working up the courage to take the risk; and having strategies ready to tolerate the anxiety associated with your proposed risk.

"Formulating plans for future action is risky bearing in mind uncertainty about the outcome. But nothing important is ever achieved without taking some risk. I can judge the risk by weighing the upside against the downside."

"If I am willing to tolerate frustration now to increase RAi tomorrow, it is a risk worth taking. If I am afraid of frustration and choose non-frustrating options today that cause dissatisfaction tomorrow, then this is a choice not worth making. I won't avoid frustration today if it causes trouble tomorrow."

From your instinct's perspective, the risk of taking action to improve your relationship is that your efforts might fail, it might get worse, and this will undermine relative importance in your own eyes or in the eyes of your family or friends. Your instinct wants you to believe that if your relative importance worsens you will not and cannot survive, and that's the worst thing that can happen. When you are calm, these conclusions are clearly irrational. When you are upset, they feel real. Chicken Little and crew are good at catastrophizing.

Once you have lowered the intensity of your emotional reaction (Step 1), and have a clear perspective of your diminished RAi (Step 2), restoration (Step 3) requires you to take action in spite of your instinct's negative comparisonitis and catastrophizing.

If you are likely to be dissatisfied with future consequences, then it's a win-lose action: achievement experienced today but not tomorrow. Satisfaction today may not be worth dissatisfaction tomorrow. If you are dissatisfied today but likely satisfied tomorrow, it's a lose-win action. But disappointment today may well be worth satisfaction tomorrow.

"If I am going to risk taking action I want to be able to determine if the risk is worthwhile. I need to define progress and need objective ways of measuring such progress."

LOVE (listen, overlook, value, effort) could be used to objectively measure the degree of relative importance in your relationship or in re-building the relative importance in your relationship. To what extent is listening, overlooking, and valuing occurring in your relationship? How much are you doing? How much is your partner doing? The answers to these questions can help you evaluate the level of relative importance existing right now in your relationship or at the time that it ended.

To restore RAi in your relationship, you have to reach a common agreement with your partner about what listening, overlooking, valuing, and effort entails. You also have to plan for more activity to occur in each of these areas in a consistent fashion.

**The cookie jar strategy requires each individual to write down five things they would like to do with their partner. Each activity is written on a separate piece of paper and then screwed up into a tight little ball. The result is ten, tight little balls of paper in a jar or glass. Someone starts the process by reaching in and drawing out a ball. It may be their own or their partner's. It does not matter.**

**The next step is that without telling the other person what activity they have picked out, they have two weeks to arrange for that activity to occur. Everything required to arrange the activity, including child minding if necessary, has to be arranged by whoever pulled out the activity. After the activity has occurred, the turn changes. Ten activities covers twenty weeks. That is a good period of time to assess whether increased RAi in your relationship will make a difference.**

In the beginning, you would not write down activities you already know your partner dislikes. You want to choose activities that you would like and that you believe your partner would also like. If you can't think of five activities that fit into this category, that's not so unusual. People's interests change. So, you will need to make some guesses. Just don't choose something that you know your partner would not like to do.

Make sure your partner doesn't know what is coming. Some of these activities can turn out to be very dissatisfying. If this occurs, you might have learned something about your partner's change in likes. Or it might occur because the universe rained on your parade when you were drinking champagne on the beach and dumped a bucket on you. Whatever the case, you are creating new memories for your relationship. You cannot know in advance whether they will be positive.

The only real downside to this activity occurs if it doesn't happen within your two-week period. Unless caused by a real-world crisis outside of your relationship, your failure to make it happen will be sending a very clear message to your partner about their importance to you and your commitment to restoration.

Once you have identified actions you can take to restore sunshine to your relationship, record the frequency and time you spend on these activities. Start recording and look for an increase in your time and effort. At least at first, don't start measuring your progress by how you feel during this risk-taking activity. Feelings change readily in response to whatever instinct is catastrophizing about in the background. You can never know whether you are going to feel satisfied, but you can know that the chances of love improving RAi in your relationship are good. Increase the amount of LOVE in your relationship and get the odds in your favor.

An important element of restorative thought is to include self-talk that motivates action and a strategy to tolerate the anxiety of taking the risk that your effort to restore RAi in your relationship might not be reciprocated.

The following thoughts are examples of restoration ideas. For them to be useful, action has to follow.

"When my partner doesn't listen to me, I understand that my instinct concludes that I am not important enough to hear. However, this conclusion only makes sense if the situation is life-and-death—like my partner had the rope, and I was drowning, and I was yelling for them to throw it, and they weren't listening. But I am not drowning, this is not life-and-death, and there are many reasons why my partner might not be hearing me, and none of them might be about me. My partner might be stewing about any number of things, including their health, work, family, or money. None of these issues has a bearing on my relative importance to my partner. These problems are not 'sky is falling' situations. Before I believe instinct, I can check with my partner to see what they are stewing about."

"It will be hard for me to focus on what I can do in my relationship and hope that this will be enough for me to get what I want: attention, validation, and approval. But that is my model. If love is evaporating in my relationship, then it is first up to me to love more, both myself and my partner. My partner's instinct is seeking attention, validation, and approval. If I provide more of it, that is all I can do to preserve my relationship. I am going to stick to my intention to focus on what I can do for myself and my partner and not on what my partner should be doing for me."

"I expect my partner to react defensively at first as their instinct will focus their attention mostly on themselves. I can hope that my unconditional efforts might trigger reciprocal RAi when my partner realizes I am not demanding anything in return. When this occurs, this is the opportunity for me to get the attention, validation, and approval that instinct needs for me to feel special in my relationship."

"If this doesn't happen enough, then eventually my relationship will fail. If it does, I have the determination and ability to survive the hurt, fear, insecurity, and anger that instinct will generate for me. I will reassure instinct that I know how to survive, and I will. I know that thinking this won't take my awful feelings away, but I can survive my feelings."

"If I notice my partner's dissatisfaction, I can respond to it with more love. But I won't take responsibility for how their instinct is affecting them. If my partner acts out dramatically, I will make clear that I disapprove of the behavior and not withdraw my validation or approval of my partner. If I have words of disapproval, I will make sure to balance my words of disapproval with words of approval."

"All of this is going to be hard for me to do, and I will need to be ready with techniques to manage my physical distress." (See Chapter 7.)

"When my partner, friend, sibling, child, or parent display their disapproval of my behavior, I will actively listen to their opinion and state my intent to consider them. First, I will do this for their benefit, so their instinct can appreciate my acknowledgement of their perspective. Making this effort is important to maintain my close relationship with them. Secondly, I will do this for my benefit; I could learn something from my consideration of the reasons they gave for their disapproval."

"The frustration of the effort to make a difference is worth it if it leads to satisfaction. Trying to avoid the frustration of this effort by choosing easy options—e.g., blaming my partner—will only cause more dissatisfaction later. Avoidance and easy options are not useful when it comes to restoration. The hard way is the only way."

**Breaking Up**

**Relationships break up when there is a critical or ongoing failure to maintain sufficient RAi. This failure can occur because of a singular event triggering an instinctive shattering of RAi, e.g., betrayal. More often, however, relationships break up as a result of repeated failure to generate and retain RAi. In either case, the relationship becomes an instinctive life-and-death scenario, and individuals first fight and then flee to survive.**

The events that trigger a reduction in relative importance can occur inside and outside the relationship. These are events that suddenly or gradually have led to high levels of frustration and dissatisfaction and have pushed individuals into the More-on Zone (Chapter 4). More-on Zone reactions then escalate irrational behavior and negativity in the relationship. The types of circumstances that can trigger More-on Zone frustration and deal-breaking relationship dissatisfaction are unique to individuals and are determined by their life history going back to childhood and including current life circumstances.

If your attempts to resuscitate your relationship have failed, and you want to declare it over, the RAi you now get from ending the relationship has to outweigh the fear and the distress of ending it. To achieve this end, you need to work on tolerating and managing your frustration and fear and generating increasing RAi for yourself.

The missing RAi that got you to this point includes being faced with the ongoing reality that you have little in common with your partner; that your partner seems to have changed; that your perception of yourself has changed from strong to weak or from independent to dependent; that your life outside of your relationship is negatively affected; that you are compromising your daily life to cater to your partner; that you have become an approval-seeker; that you are limiting the satisfying activities in your life to appease a failing relationship; that your one and only chance to be happy in a relationship is gone; that you are getting older by the minute.

Typical fears include your partner blaming you, not understanding you, frightening you, yelling at you, threatening you, breaking down, threatening self-harm. You will likely worry about financial security, how the breakup will impact your friends, your parents, your work, your business. You will worry about ever finding the "right" partner and whether you will ever have children. If you already have children, you will worry about child support and how the breakup will affect them—grieving for a lost parent, having to take sides, relationships with their friends, losing role models. In broader terms, you will worry about how it will affect the RAi you get from the wider community, how you will be seen by others now that your relationship has ended.

**So, what do you do?**

- Make frustration more tolerable through activities to reduce its intensity.
- Focus on changing your behavior before you concentrate on improving others' and your life circumstances.
- Normalize your comparisonitis and catastrophizing so that you don't misinterpret your bad feelings to mean that you are making a terrible mistake.
- Use restoration activities to generate your own RAi independent of the external conditions.

"My partner's aggressive behavior directed at themselves or me is caused by their survival instinct trying to preserve their relative importance. Nevertheless, my instinct will take it personally and will catastrophize about the disrespect I am receiving. I should expect that and remind myself of the RAi I will get from ending this."

"The idea that my children will be permanently affected by this breakup is an example of instinct's catastrophizing. It does upset me, and if it were true, it should. Yet there is no evidence to support this idea. My fear is based on instinct's catastrophizing, not on reality."

"On occasions when I might be confident about my decision, I won't be surprised when instinct spoils it. I should expect that any satisfaction that I get from going ahead with this will start to deteriorate when instinct winds me up again and catastrophizes about my future. I have to remember that satisfaction fluctuates because instinct doesn't allow for it to last."

"If I accept the necessity of feeling bad about this breakup, I can stop trying to avoid it and focus more on thinking about what my restoration steps will be and what the outcomes are that I want. Yes, what's happening seems awful and terrible and unfair, but it is what it is. What is my next activity, and how will it add to my sense of RAi if I take it? Will I approve of my actions, and will the consequences of my actions be useful?"

Effective behavior when relationships struggle is based on your ability to release your frustration when things are dissatisfying and on your determination to see the behavior of your partner, friend, sibling, child, or parent not as evidence of how they feel about you, but as evidence of how they are feeling about themselves. To be happy in spite of the comparisonitis and catastrophizing of your instinct, you need to be able not to take things too personally. When RAi from your partner diminishes, it is more useful to think that your partner is going through a "sky is falling" moment with their insecurity and fear because of the 84,000 things outside of your relationship.

The strategy that sustains intimate relationships is based on the idea that you get what you want from your partner by giving that same exact thing to your partner in their language. Your partner's instinct has the same goal that yours has: to survive. What's important to you is likewise important to your partner, but its expression will be different.

Your strategy is to discover through risk-taking and action learning how to increase your partner's sense of validation and approval and make it happen. At the same time, to generate RAi for yourself, you need to be clear about what you want from your partner to feel validated and approved of. You don't need to get what you want; just expressing it is enough to generate RAi for yourself. Take the step of being clear about what you want, but stop short of demanding this. When demands are made, people mostly feel criticized, disapproved of, and by comparison, less important. This is likely how your partner will feel if you are having a Chicken Little moment and start demanding with "sky is falling" behavior.

**Summary.**

**Having successful intimate relationships requires ongoing use of cPR:**

- **Keep a rough check on your day-to-day RAi sensitivities and the dissatisfaction they cause.**
- **If you are not getting enough RAi, take responsibility to top it up yourself and look for opportunities to increase the RAi you shine on your partner. LOVE your partner.**

- **Don't take it too personally if your RAi is one-sided. This is not a reflection on you. It is a reflection of the 84,000 things impacting on your partner. Seek an understanding of these, talk to your partner, listen, and value.**
- **Start the game of *Relationship Snakes and Ladders*.**

**Establishing a habit.**

A habit is established when feelings, thoughts, and actions move from the deliberate to the unconscious. At this point, they begin to occur pretty much without you realizing it. You create a habit by deliberately repeating behavior until it becomes automatic. You create a habit by playing *Snakes and Ladders* (also known in the US as the popular board game *Chutes and Ladders*).

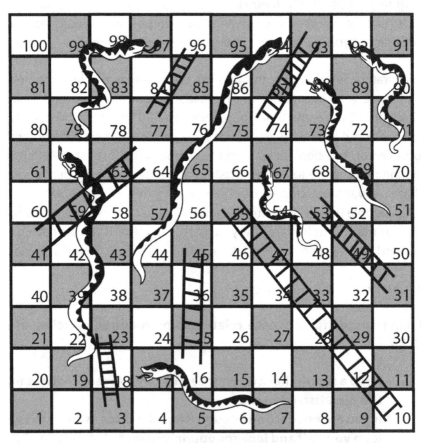

*Snakes and Ladders* board game

According to the Museum of Gaming Newsletter 2 from February 2015, *Snakes and Ladders* originated in ancient India as *Moksha Patam*, and it was tied to the Hindu philosophies of karma, fate based on one's actions, and samskara, rites of passage.

In the board game, the snakes create unhappiness by jumping you backward, while the ladders create happiness by jumping you forward. You move by throwing a die, and you win by reaching the end first. You can see the snakes and ladders before you reach them, but the outcome is one of pure luck with no real skill or strategy.

If you envision *Snakes and Ladders* as a game of life, the snakes also create unhappiness by jumping you backwards, while the ladders create happiness by jumping you forwards. But in the game of life, you don't roll the die; you can only move by generating RAi. You don't win by reaching the end first; you win by being happy, and to do that you have to keep moving. You can't see the snakes or the ladders before you reach them. You need to make assumptions about whether a move will lead to a snake or a ladder, but you can never be sure. In this game, pure luck can produce RAi, but it is not the only source of RAi. You can also produce it for yourself both directly (LOVE yourself) and indirectly (LOVE others), and this is where the skill and strategy comes in.

As a game of life, there is no balance in *Snakes and Ladders*, and there are more snakes than ladders. Reality is what it is. To win at *Life Snakes and Ladders* requires LOVE and cPR and your progress to become habitual. You use LOVE and the RAi it produces to move, and cPR to cope with "snakes." The development of these habits is one of the most important and rewarding things you can do.

# Relationship Snakes and Ladders Calendar

# August

| | | 1 | 2 | 3 | 4 | 5 |
|---|---|---|---|---|---|---|
| □ Pure Luck<br>□ Direct RAi<br>□ Indirect RAi | □ Pure Luck<br>□ Direct RAi<br>□ Indirect RAi | □ Pure Luck<br>□ Direct RAi<br>□ Indirect RAi | □ Pure Luck<br>□ Direct RAi<br>□ Indirect RAi | □ Pure Luck<br>□ Direct RAi<br>□ Indirect RAi | □ Pure Luck<br>□ Direct RAi<br>□ Indirect RAi | □ Pure Luck<br>□ Direct RAi<br>□ Indirect RAi |
| 6 | 7 | 8 | 9 | 10 | 11 | 12 |
| □ Pure Luck<br>□ Direct RAi<br>□ Indirect RAi | □ Pure Luck<br>□ Direct RAi<br>□ Indirect RAi | □ Pure Luck<br>□ Direct RAi<br>□ Indirect RAi | □ Pure Luck<br>□ Direct RAi<br>□ Indirect RAi | □ Pure Luck<br>□ Direct RAi<br>□ Indirect RAi | □ Pure Luck<br>□ Direct RAi<br>□ Indirect RAi | □ Pure Luck<br>□ Direct RAi<br>□ Indirect RAi |
| 13 | 14 | 15 | 16 | 17 | 18 | 19 |
| □ Pure Luck<br>□ Direct RAi<br>□ Indirect RAi | □ Pure Luck<br>□ Direct RAi<br>□ Indirect RAi | □ Pure Luck<br>□ Direct RAi<br>□ Indirect RAi | □ Pure Luck<br>□ Direct RAi<br>□ Indirect RAi | □ Pure Luck<br>□ Direct RAi<br>□ Indirect RAi | □ Pure Luck<br>□ Direct RAi<br>□ Indirect RAi | □ Pure Luck<br>□ Direct RAi<br>□ Indirect RAi |
| 20 | 21 | 22 | 23 | 24 | 25 | 26 |
| □ Pure Luck<br>□ Direct RAi<br>□ Indirect RAi | □ Pure Luck<br>□ Direct RAi<br>□ Indirect RAi | □ Pure Luck<br>□ Direct RAi<br>□ Indirect RAi | □ Pure Luck<br>□ Direct RAi<br>□ Indirect RAi | □ Pure Luck<br>□ Direct RAi<br>□ Indirect RAi | □ Pure Luck<br>□ Direct RAi<br>□ Indirect RAi | □ Pure Luck<br>□ Direct RAi<br>□ Indirect RAi |
| 27 | 28 | 29 | 30 | 31 | | |
| □ Pure Luck<br>□ Direct RAi<br>□ Indirect RAi | □ Pure Luck<br>□ Direct RAi<br>□ Indirect RAi | □ Pure Luck<br>□ Direct RAi<br>□ Indirect RAi | □ Pure Luck<br>□ Direct RAi<br>□ Indirect RAi | □ Pure Luck<br>□ Direct RAi<br>□ Indirect RAi | □ Pure Luck<br>□ Direct RAi<br>□ Indirect RAi | □ Pure Luck<br>□ Direct RAi<br>□ Indirect RAi |

Relationship Snakes and Ladders
Calendar

**First Move.**

You need RAi to move. There are three ways to get it.

- Luck—You happen to be in the right place at the right time with the right mix of attributes (looks, intelligence, vulnerability, money, availability) to collect a blast of RAi from the universe and the people in it. Your survival instinct is constantly on the lookout for these opportunities (and threats). That's what happened to Nick and Emily on the night of the party.

- Indirectly—You generate RAi by LOVEing others. (You hope, but had better not expect, that you will get some RAi in return. Demandingness is certain to dry up any source of RAi.) LOVEing others means noticing and making time for them, accepting and tolerating their shortcomings, and valuing them with something that you believe is important to them.
- Directly—You generate RAi by LOVEing yourself. You notice and make time for yourself, you accept and forgive your shortcomings, and you value yourself with something that is important to you.

**Second Move.**

You need RAi. There are three ways to get it.

**Third Move.**

You need RAi. There are three ways to get it.

By now you can see that repetition is required to play *Snakes and Ladders*. If you don't deliberately create RAi each day, you stop moving. You can only be happy if you are moving. Below you will see an example of a *Snakes and Ladders* calendar that you could use to establish a habit of generating RAi.

Each day has three boxes representing the three ways of experiencing RAi. Tick any box if it applies to your day. You only need to tick one box to enable you to move. If you have qualified to move, put a big cross (or tick) on the day.

**Landing on a Snake.**

This will happen when something *bad* happens in the Luck box or Indirect box. You might have worried about it happening in advance, but you never really know it will happen until it does. When it happens, you do not slide backwards in your progress; your progress just stops. You miss a turn. On this day, your chain stops. This is not a catastrophe. You simply start again on the day after. You do not go back to the beginning of the month. The longer your chain, the stronger your sense of satisfaction and happiness.

Life will dump a snake on you that may prevent you from ticking any of the three boxes and will cause the chain to break. This will happen, and it is what it is. As former Australian Prime Minister Malcolm Fraser once said, "Life wasn't meant to be easy." He later went on to refer to the full quotation from *Back to Methuselah* by George Bernard Shaw: "Life wasn't meant to be easy, my child; but take courage: it can be glorious." That's where ladders come in.

Until you can restore your RAi you are stuck. You are not qualified to make a move. This is the time to put your attention on your Direct box and generate RAi for yourself. Remember, you do that by LOVEing yourself, by using the strategy of cPR.

Filling out your calendar each day takes your focus off being stuck and creates a habit of moving forward. If you are moving, you will be satisfied, content, and even happy (if RAi is high enough to enter your Happiness Zone). Your good feelings will last as long as you keep moving.

If a day goes by and you can't tick any of the three boxes, this is not a catastrophe. Your chain of movement stops at this point, that is all. You start again the next day, tick a box, make a move and start building your next chain. As you continue this process, your chains will get longer and longer and you build reserves of RAi, and satisfaction.

**Landing on a Ladder.**

This will happen when something unexpected and *good* happens in the Luck box or in the Indirect box. You may plan for good things to happen, but you don't really benefit from it until it does. When it does, your RAi has a burst of intensity, you feel great. If your RAi level hits the happiness zone, you will be happy. You have definitely qualified to make your next move, but once again, you don't know if your happiness will last, and you don't have expectations one way or the other.

# Relationship Snakes and Ladders Calendar

## August

| | | 1 | 2 | 3 | 4 | 5 |
|---|---|---|---|---|---|---|
| ☐ Pure Luck<br>☐ Direct RAi<br>☐ Indirect RAi | ☐ Pure Luck<br>☐ Direct RAi<br>☐ Indirect RAi | ☐ Pure Luck<br>☐ Direct RAi<br>☐ Indirect RAi | ☐ Pure Luck<br>☐ Direct RAi<br>☐ Indirect RAi | ☐ Pure Luck<br>☐ Direct RAi<br>☐ Indirect RAi | ☐ Pure Luck<br>☐ Direct RAi<br>☐ Indirect RAi | ☐ Pure Luck<br>☐ Direct RAi<br>☐ Indirect RAi |
| 6 | 7 | 8 | 9 | 10 | 11 | 12 |
| ☐ Pure Luck<br>☐ Direct RAi<br>☐ Indirect RAi | ☐ Pure Luck<br>☐ Direct RAi<br>☐ Indirect RAi | ☐ Pure Luck<br>☐ Direct RAi<br>☐ Indirect RAi | ☐ Pure Luck<br>☐ Direct RAi<br>☐ Indirect RAi | ☐ Pure Luck<br>☐ Direct RAi<br>☐ Indirect RAi | ☐ Pure Luck<br>☐ Direct RAi<br>☐ Indirect RAi | ☐ Pure Luck<br>☐ Direct RAi<br>☐ Indirect RAi |
| 13 | 14 | 15 | 16 | 17 | 18 | 19 |
| ☐ Pure Luck<br>☐ Direct RAi<br>☐ Indirect RAi | ☐ Pure Luck<br>☐ Direct RAi<br>☐ Indirect RAi | ☐ Pure Luck<br>☐ Direct RAi<br>☐ Indirect RAi | ☐ Pure Luck<br>☐ Direct RAi<br>☐ Indirect RAi | ☐ Pure Luck<br>☐ Direct RAi<br>☐ Indirect RAi | ☐ Pure Luck<br>☐ Direct RAi<br>☐ Indirect RAi | ☐ Pure Luck<br>☐ Direct RAi<br>☐ Indirect RAi |
| 20 | 21 | 22 | 23 | 24 | 25 | 26 |
| ☐ Pure Luck<br>☐ Direct RAi<br>☐ Indirect RAi | ☐ Pure Luck<br>☐ Direct RAi<br>☐ Indirect RAi | ☐ Pure Luck<br>☐ Direct RAi<br>☐ Indirect RAi | ☐ Pure Luck<br>☐ Direct RAi<br>☐ Indirect RAi | ☐ Pure Luck<br>☐ Direct RAi<br>☐ Indirect RAi | ☐ Pure Luck<br>☐ Direct RAi<br>☐ Indirect RAi | ☐ Pure Luck<br>☐ Direct RAi<br>☐ Indirect RAi |
| 27 | 28 | 29 | 30 | 31 | | |
| ☐ Pure Luck<br>☐ Direct RAi<br>☐ Indirect RAi | ☐ Pure Luck<br>☐ Direct RAi<br>☐ Indirect RAi | ☐ Pure Luck<br>☐ Direct RAi<br>☐ Indirect RAi | ☐ Pure Luck<br>☐ Direct RAi<br>☐ Indirect RAi | ☐ Pure Luck<br>☐ Direct RAi<br>☐ Indirect RAi | ☐ Pure Luck<br>☐ Direct RAi<br>☐ Indirect RAi | ☐ Pure Luck<br>☐ Direct RAi<br>☐ Indirect RAi |

If it is to be then it is up to me as well as the snakes and the ladders.

# CHAPTER 9
# PARENTING

Emily still meets with a handful of moms from her antenatal class. They get together once a month and share their experiences as mothers. The moms have a coffee while the kids are gradually interacting and playing with each other. Compared to the other kids, Jake is slow. Well, he is not the slowest, but he lags the most with his words. Even though he was a solid kid from the beginning, he was also almost the last to start walking, and he is a bit rough. If he wants a toy, he just takes it. He doesn't seem to care if the other kids cry, and once when another boy took his block, Jake whacked him. There have been times when Emily got so stressed about going that she didn't want to go. But Emily is not a quitter, and she goes for Jake.

There are many "shoulds" and "should nots" underlying Emily's distress and her frustration with Jake. She worries that Jake is not developing as he should and that he is behaving in ways that he shouldn't. She worries that she is doing something wrong as a parent. Emily is also pretty sure that she is being judged by at least some of the other mothers. Before the kids were born, Emily was the go-to source of information in the group on supplements, exercise, breathing techniques. After all, Emily had graduated and worked as a solicitor before pregnancy, and the other girls were pretty impressed by that.

She now feels that her status in the group has shifted from being an insider to an outsider. She feels that she has lost the group's approval, and rather than being important to the group, she is now a source of irritation to the group. If she could just control Jake, but Jake is just such a challenging kid. Emily sort of blames Nick. Jake has the same rebellious and independent nature that Nick has. Although she reminds herself that this is one of the things she loves about Nick, Emily knows Jake's behavior isn't popular with the others. Emily feels that the other mothers don't want him there, that they think she should have taught him better manners, and that Jake should behave better toward the other kids.

Remember the Chicken Little story? When things happen in parenting situations that your instinct deems to be of life-and-death importance, you will experience increasingly negative physical reactions that promote unconscious and then conscious catastrophizing. Unless you expose your "shoulds" and reality test them, your instinct can lead to the very outcomes that you were not expecting—in this case being unhappy with parenthood and even sometimes not liking your own kids.

There is a fair amount of agreement on what the parenting job involves. Raise your kids to be responsible. That is, *response-able* to tolerate and make the most of the ups and downs their future will bring. What you have learned to be valuable from your life experience and the opinions of the "experts" mostly agree. Kids need to be noticed and valued. They need to feel important. They need to feel safe, loved, protected. From this base of security, they need to be willing to try and to be able to cope regardless of the outcome of whatever they do. They need to learn that if they want something, then it is up to them to get it.

"If it is to be, then it is up to me."

To do this, they need to have practice with exposure to success, to disappointment, and the consequences of both. Resilience does not grow from gain alone; it has to include learning to tolerate exposure to pain.

Parenting is a challenging activity because children don't acquire what it takes to be response-able primarily from talks, lectures, or lessons. These are good to have. But the learning of how to be responsible that sinks in for children comes from them observing behavior, not from listening to words. It's the "walk" and not the "talk" that really influences our kids, and the fact is, modeling response-able behavior for our children to observe can be hard and sometimes impossible to do in the face of our frustration, dissatisfaction, and unhappiness.

*Dr. Robert Dawson*

Parenting is also a challenging activity because of the many instinctive conflicts that occur. The over-arching purpose of instinct is survival of the human species. If this big picture was a jigsaw puzzle, then the pieces of the puzzle in the context of parenting would relate to the survival of each parent as well as the child.

Instinct equates our survival chances to the degree to which we are noticed, approved of, and valued. From our instinct's perspective, if we are noticed, we are safe. If we are valued, we are safe. Each parent wants to be noticed and valued, and each child wants to be noticed and valued. How can everyone be noticed and valued at the same time? Moreover, each parent and child instinctively pursue these outcomes in each different aspect of their life. How does anyone get approval from everybody even some of the time—let alone all the time—in all arenas?

As a parent, you have found yourself disciplining your child in the midst of disapproval from your partner, family, friends, strangers, or even politicians. How frustrating is that? How difficult is it to stick to your ideas and values when you are disciplining (or not disciplining) in the face of others' disapproval? How much doubt does that cause you? How many times do you switch methods in the face of your uncertainty and desire to do the best for your kids while at the same time be seen by the wider community as a good parent.

No matter how good you are at multi-tasking, it is simply not possible to notice and value everyone in the family at the same time while having your parenting approved by everyone around you. Someone is going to feel under-valued (and often enough it is you); someone is going to have a different idea about what you should be doing, and eventually you are going to sense their disapproval. When this occurs, your instinct is going to make you feel frustrated, dissatisfied, and maybe unhappy.

**Rubber Meets the Road.**

To increase your confidence and satisfaction as a parent:

- Start by getting clear about what you want to achieve. What sort of an adult you want your child to become? Judge the usefulness of your parenting from this perspective. Remember that what kids see is more important than what they hear. Reflect on what your children see you doing and what they might learn from that. Also, make sure you are aware of, and ask questions about, what they see other people doing at school, on TV, on social media, on the internet, and what they might be learning from that.

- Look for the unconscious "shoulds" and "should nots" that are creating your frustration and undermining your RAi.
- Reality test and replace these thoughts with a perspective that allows you to get what you want (less frustration) and restore your RAi (more satisfaction).

Frustration and diminished RAi only occur when things are not the way they should be. So, ask yourself:

- What are my frustrations when I am parenting? Look for the "shoulds" or "should nots" creating your frustration when things don't happen the way they should.
- What are the "shoulds" or "should nots" that determine my recognition, approval, and importance as a parent?

**As a rule, try not to "should" on yourself or anyone else. The fewer the number of "shoulds" (or "should nots") in your life, the better for you and the better for others.**

Typical frustrations include tiredness, not getting enough help, and the repetitive nature of cooking, feeding, cleaning, and changing. These activities have moments of pleasure, surprise, excitement, and laughter. But there is boredom and frustration there as well. The major "shoulds" here are the ones about getting more help. Parents are on the job and on call twenty-four hours a day.

Disciplining is another major source of frustration. As there is no universally accepted step-by-step parenting manual, you won't ever know exactly what you should do in each situation. Instinct wants to know what you should and should not be doing, and everyone around you has an opinion on that. You are going to get disapproval from somebody no matter what you do. It's pretty frustrating to be damned if you do and damned if you don't. It is also emotionally stressful to live day to day with an underlying worry about having done the right thing for your child.

"There should be a manual," says your instinct.

What are the "shoulds" that define your recognition, approval, and importance as a parent? Your instinct seeks RAi just like your kids and your partner do. When all your effort is being focused on your children and your partner, your instinct begins to feel insecure, unnoticed, taken for granted, and unimportant. You are frequently putting them first; you should get recognition for this huge effort.

Satisfaction with your life and your parenting role diminishes as your instinct's insecurity increases. You need to understand this is a normal reaction. If you don't, you will get frustrated with yourself for feeling dissatisfied. You will find yourself thinking:

> "After all, it shouldn't be about me; it should be about my kids."

> "What's wrong with me? I have two beautiful and healthy kids. I should be happy."

> "How selfish am I, making it all about me."

Satisfaction will also be diminished by judgments about how you have handled things—specifically how you have put your need for RAi or relief from frustration ahead of your partner's or your children's needs. Guilt is a constant factor undermining satisfaction as a parent.

Satisfaction in your parenting role will increase as your kids grow up and become the adults you want them to be. In the meantime, over the 20 or more years that it takes for this to happen, your RAi is going to take quite a beating unless you make time for yourself and take care of yourself.

If you want to be happy parenting in spite of:

- A lack of a parenting manual.
- A fear of teaching your kids the wrong thing.
- A feeling of being a failure.
- A fear of disapproval.
- A feeling of losing yourself.
- A feeling of being judged and unsupported by others.

you need to become aware of the "shoulds" and "should nots" that actually undermine your recognition, approval, and importance. Expect and normalize the collateral damage caused by your instinct's comparisonitis and catastrophizing "shoulds" in search of more and more RAi. Remember that from instinct's perspective, you can never, ever have enough RAi. Moderate using instinct's "should" approach to generate RAi by instead generating it for yourself with cPR.

**Psychological Resuscitation.**

**Step 1 of cPR: Calming Frustration.**

While the perspective and restoration required to resuscitate happiness will be different from situation to situation, achieving small *c*, a little bit of calm, is the first and necessary step regardless of the situation. Movement and distraction are great activities for attaining small *c*; see Chapter 7 for details on getting small *c* and to remind yourself of the risks of drug use.

**Step 2 of cPR: Perspective on RAi.**

Emily can search the three dimensions of RAi to better understand her distressing perspective of her ability as a parent. She needs to ask questions of herself.

The first question is about being noticed:

- *Am I sensitive about recognition in my role as a mother?*

"In antenatal class, everyone was interested in what I had to say. Now they barely listen to my opinions. After all, Jake is hardly a billboard for great ways to bring up your kid."

The second question is about approval:

- *Am I sensitive about the approval I am getting as a mother?*

"I can see the way the other mothers look at Jake and go to great lengths to protect their kids from him. Monica even lost it at our last group meeting and told me I should make Jake share his toys. Nick told me not to let Jake get away with snatching blocks from Abbey. It's not my fault. Jake is a good kid. He's just independent and a little defiant. I don't want to squash that spirit in him. As long as he isn't hurting anything, he should be able to express that spirit."

The third question is about importance:

- *Am I sensitive about no longer being important to the group and being regarded by Nick as not being a good mother?*

"The group used to ask me what I think. Hardly anyone does that anymore, and I have to volunteer my opinion if I want it to be heard. Nick mostly praises me for the job I am doing for the kids, but there are occasions when he overrules me in front of them. He shouldn't undermine my authority in front of them. It encourages them to do the same."

You have to first bring these thoughts to the surface before you can moderate the collateral damage that they cause.

**"To learn the secrets of life, we must first become aware of them." (Albert Einstein)**

Below are examples of surfaced thoughts that, once identified, can be normalized to moderate instinct's sensitivity to perceived loss of RAi in the parenting role.

You may identify with some of them. You don't need to find all of your instinct's comparisonitis and catastrophizing. All you need to do is to identify a small number of clear thoughts that highlight instinct's fears. The work we do with a few will generalize to all of them and prepare us to move on to restoration.

Examples:

"My goal as a parent is for my kids to grow up to be response-able adults, to have the ability to cope with whatever comes their way. I believe that the way to achieve this outcome is to focus more on showing them than telling them. I want to show them how I enjoy satisfaction and how I tolerate frustration. I won't always do well in these demonstrations, and I want to show that if I don't handle things well, that's still OK."

"I understand that much of their behavior will be driven by their instinct's need to be noticed, approved of, and protected. I will try not to take their negative behavior personally, as a reflection on me as a mother. So, when I am allowing them to experience distress, not taking it personally will ensure that my attention is off me and onto them, that they have my approval, and that they are safe."

"I understand that instinct will react to others' disapproval of my parenting as a drop in my relative importance. It sees this as a survival threat and pushes me to seek the attention and approval of other people to raise my relative importance. But I can tolerate others' disapproval. In spite of my instinct's fears, I will survive."

"When my kids are fighting, I will see this as a clash of their instincts and not a clash of the values they have learned. I will try to stay out of these fights and allow them to experience the emotional pain of conflict. I manage my own distress to allow me to tolerate theirs."

> **Depriving your kids of the opportunity for favorite activities is a time-tested, effective consequence for the behavior you want to see less of. Deprivation will reduce the frequency of unwanted behavior sooner or later. Note that nothing will totally eliminate unwanted behavior. Your kids have survival instincts the same as you do, and under sufficiently threatening conditions, instinct rules. Aim to reduce, not totally eliminate, unwanted behavior in your children.**
>
> **Deprivation might work right away; it might take some time to work. It will work if you apply it consistently. Try not to start with long deprivation intervals (e.g., phone, ball, bike, being confiscated for a month). Start with short intervals and gradually increase the deprivation time until you get the result you want.**

> Deprivation won't work at all if you cannot control your children's access to favorite activities. Deprivation doesn't work with teenagers and adults unless you can totally control their access to attention and approval. Good luck with that.
>
> Timeouts are also an effective consequence for unwanted behavior as long as timeout means total disconnection from attention and approval. Make sure that the location of timeout does mean isolation and does not allow access to social media (computers, phones, tablets). Start with a timeout interval equal to the child's age in minutes. A twelve-year-old's timeout equals 12 minutes; three years old equals three minutes. If that isn't working after some trials, gradually increase the time. This time might seem short to you. The disconnection caused by the timeout does not need to be a long interval to be effective. Human survival instinct is very needy.

"It is going to be hard for me to do this, and I will need to be ready with techniques to manage my physiological distress. I would like my child to learn how to cope with distress by observing me coping with my distress."

"If I am exposing myself to frustration in search of satisfaction, then the frustration is worth it. If I am trying to avoid frustration by choosing easy options that produce future dissatisfaction, then avoiding frustration is not worth it. I won't pursue my parenting goals through actions that cause dissatisfaction in the future."

These thoughts are examples of reaching an awareness of what is happening first at an unconscious level in the limbic system and then at a conscious level in the frontal lobe.

**Step 3 of cPR: Restoration of RAi**

Perspective on missing RAi will normalize instinct's catastrophizing and prepare you for the goal of restoration. Restoration of satisfaction and happiness when faced with the difficulty of parenting requires you to:

- Restore recognition.
- Restore approval.
- Restore importance.

Restoration requires:

- An openness for action.
- A willingness to take risks.
- A determination to learn from outcomes.
- An ability to improvise and adapt.

Dealing with unwanted circumstances can lead to such intense levels of frustration that you readily get to the point of giving up. If you get stopped by your bad feelings, you can get moving again by following the restoration routine of risk-taking and action learning.

Effective risk-taking requires you to:

- Assess the possible consequences of your actions before you take them.
- Put a value on the worthiness of the risk.
- Work up the courage to take the risk.
- Have in place strategies to tolerate the anxiety associated with the proposed risk.

A method of measuring the value of a risk is to estimate the balance between the anxiety of taking the risk (the downside) and the future satisfaction from taking the risk (the upside). If you are likely to be satisfied with the future consequences of your action, and you can tolerate the frustration, it's worth taking. If you are likely to be dissatisfied with future consequences, then it's not worth taking. Even if you are satisfied now, you need to think about future satisfaction. Satisfaction today is not worth dissatisfaction tomorrow.

You don't require a crystal ball to evaluate risks. All you need do is take some time and think about possible future consequences. Action learning requires a definition of success and a means of objective measurement of progress. It requires a focus on acquiring the skills needed for development, the motivation to practice these skills, and the openness to keep adapting efforts in the face of objective evidence.

The restoration ideas and strategies that you plan and put into action only need a possibility of success. You are not going to come up with a plan that guarantees minimum frustration, satisfaction, confidence, and happiness, because 84,000 things in your environment will continue to affect the outcome. This means that no matter how carefully you plan for an outcome, something may still go wrong.

> **Reactive parenting focuses on giving your child a childhood—*"just let them be kids"*—and on protecting them as much as possible from experiencing distress. Strategic parenting is focused on teaching your child what they need to be successful in life, sports, relationships, work, and so on.**
>
> **Excessive emphasis on either approach is not likely to produce resilient, response-able adults. It is easy to make a mistake thinking that your parenting can start off with the reactive approach and switch to the strategic approach when you deem your child ready to grasp the complexity of situations and cope with responsibility and distress. This doesn't work.**
>
> **If you want your kids to be response-able, your parenting needs to be a mix of reactive and strategic right from the beginning. Providing a "circle of security" for your kids is paramount for their survival now and for their sense of security as adults. However, within this circle, you want to demonstrate for them how to think about the difference between wants and needs; about effort, costs, and consequences; and to act accordingly. Kids have the ability to learn the complexity of wants, needs, effort, costs, and consequences through watching. It's called *vicarious learning*. They do this all their lives, and they start doing it before they can speak. Your children need to be given the opportunity to learn about wants, needs, efforts, costs, and consequences way before they become teenagers.**

> A child who has learned to tolerate their own reactivity and respond strategically becomes a response-able adult. It is hard to get this outcome from your kids. Each day, you face the obstacles of your uncertainty about what to do; the potentially debilitating impact of your More-on Zone on your patience, tolerance, and skill even when you do know what to do; and the potential disapproval of others no matter what you do.

As is the case with intimate relationships, LOVE is an important restoration strategy to use when you are worrying and dissatisfied as a parent. Being happy in spite of the normal uncertainty about doing the right thing for your kids requires lots of LOVEing yourself. Being able to follow through with the difficult task of allowing your kids to learn response-ability requires lots of deliberately LOVEing them.

**Remember that any restoration strategy requires you to first calm yourself down a bit. (See Chapter 7.)**

**L**—will be actively listening to your kids when they are struggling and showing that you hear them by confirming what they mean. (You don't have to agree with them, but you do want to confirm what they are saying.) Younger kids (and sometimes teenagers and adults) often won't be able to say what they mean when they are upset. Expect that sometimes they won't be able to rationally say what they mean. On these occasions, you confirm what you think they might be saying. Confirmation (saying what you heard) conveys RAi. Oh, and be careful not to tell them what they mean when they don't know what they mean. Your frustration might prompt you to do that. Don't; it doesn't help. This is not promoting response-ability.

**O**—will be overlooking your own tendency to take things personally, as well as overlooking your kids' tendency to take things personally. Instinct makes you and your kids take things personally. When your kids are naughty in public, the judgments you can see in the eyes of onlookers suggest to your instinct that you are now a terrible human being not worthy of being supported. Unless you look, you won't see the 84,000 things behind their judgments. When you tell your child you can't afford to buy them a new phone, their instinct will be telling them that you don't love them, you don't care about them, they will be rejected by their friends because of their current crappy phone, and that their life is over. Later their "all about me" will turn into "all about you" as their anger turns you into a monster. This is all normal stuff and needs to be overlooked. Neither you or your child is a monster. This is merely instinct at work.

**V**—stands for valuing. When you do things that you believe are important, you generate RAi for yourself. When you support your kids trying out things they think are important, you generate RAi for them. There will be occasions when your opinion on what is important is not shared by your child. When this conflict occurs, you err on the side of caution, on your life experience and wisdom, and on the fact that you are the parent. When your child reacts negatively and strongly, you overlook. As your children's life experience grows, it is important that you value them by supporting their decisions more. Unwanted consequences are tough on you and your kids. But consequences are the only way to teach response-ability.

**E**—stands for effort, consistency of effort. The tough job of parenting does get easier (I didn't say easy) with deliberate effort. Regular use of cPR can make you very good at using it even without you realizing how good you are. When it becomes habitual, you may not notice that you are using cPR, but your kids and partner will, and without being able to put a finger on why, you will be happier and more confident as a parent.

Once you have identified sources of RAi, take note of the frequency and time you spend in these activities. Start measuring and look for an increase in your time and effort. Feelings change readily given that instinct is busy with comparing and catastrophizing in the background. You can never know whether you are going to feel satisfied on each occasion, but you can learn and adapt. Increase the frequency of activities that seem to attract RAi and get the odds of increased satisfaction and potential happiness in your favor.

The following thoughts are examples of restoration ideas. For them to be useful, action has to follow.

"I won't shield them from any consequences of their actions—including my occasional display of not tolerating frustration—unless a consequence is life-threatening. As much as I want them to feel good, enjoy their childhoods, and not experience distress, I know that allowing them to feel bad is the only way for them to develop resilience: the ability to tolerate feeling bad and get on with it despite feeling bad."

"Their need to be noticed will occasionally happen at a time when my attention is elsewhere. When this occurs, I expect their behavior to become increasingly dramatic. I will try to respond when I have finished my current task, rather than when their dramatic behavior demands. When this escalates into even more drama, as I know it will on occasions, I need to respond to the behavior and not to the rightness or wrongness of the behavior. I will focus on what my child did rather than on whether they should have done it. I don't want to "should" on my child. I want to show that my approval is not affected by my disapproval of their behavior."

"It will be hard for me to allow my kids to experience the distressful consequences of their actions. But that is the way resilient adults are made, and I am going to stick to my intention to allow it. When they are hurting, I will allow them to hurt, but I will keep them safe. When I respond to dramatic behavior, I will make clear my disapproval is about the behavior and not about them."

"I will make sure I balance my words of disapproval with words of approval. I will try to ensure that any physical actions I engage in with the child are positive and will focus these actions on the child (hugs, grooming, rubbing, any reassuring physical interaction)."

"On occasions when I fail to behave as intended, I will eventually say sorry (when I realize I was wrong and when I am able), admit to getting it wrong, and not use blame as an excuse for my behavior. This is the way I would like my child to behave in the future."

"When other people display their disapproval of my parenting, I will not outwardly respond. If I am connected to them in some way (family, friends), or if the situation demands an outward response, I will acknowledge their thoughts and state my intent to consider them. I will do this for their benefit, so their instinct can appreciate my acknowledgement of their perspective. And I will only make this effort if I care about them in some way and want an ongoing positive relationship with them. I might also benefit from a consideration of the reasons given for their disapproval. This is how I would like my child to respond to disapproval from others."

"When my child comes to me with a request, I want to encourage my child to think about a plan of action and consequences. I can do this by wondering aloud how that might be achieved, what the costs of the effort might be, and what the consequences of the effort might be. I want my child to adopt the approach that 'if it is to be, then it's up to me.' I want my child to think about the effort required to achieve the desired outcome and the costs and consequences of such effort."

**Summary.**

**Doing well in the parenting role requires:**

- **A clear picture of the outcome and how to get it. How effective do you want your child to be in managing whatever life brings them? Having a clear intention allows your parenting to be both strategic and reactive.**
- **Using a mix of both reactive and strategic approaches and modifying the mix as your children grow.**
- **Starting the game of *Parenting Snakes and Ladders*.**

*Parenting Snakes and Ladders*

If you haven't read about *Snakes and Ladders* as a game of life in Chapter 8, take a look now. It's at the end of the chapter.

# Parenting Snakes and Ladders Calendar
## August

| | | | | | | |
|---|---|---|---|---|---|---|
| ☐ Pure Luck<br>☐ Direct RAi<br>☐ Indirect RAi | ☐ Pure Luck<br>☐ Direct RAi<br>☐ Indirect RAi | ☐ Pure Luck<br>☐ Direct RAi<br>☐ Indirect RAi | ☐ Pure Luck<br>☐ Direct RAi<br>☐ Indirect RAi | ☐ Pure Luck<br>☐ Direct RAi<br>☐ Indirect RAi | ☐ Pure Luck<br>☐ Direct RAi<br>☐ Indirect RAi | ☐ Pure Luck<br>☐ Direct RAi<br>☐ Indirect RAi |
| **6** | **7** | **8** | **9** | **10** | **11** | **12** |
| ☐ Pure Luck<br>☐ Direct RAi<br>☐ Indirect RAi | ☐ Pure Luck<br>☐ Direct RAi<br>☐ Indirect RAi | ☐ Pure Luck<br>☐ Direct RAi<br>☐ Indirect RAi | ☐ Pure Luck<br>☐ Direct RAi<br>☐ Indirect RAi | ☐ Pure Luck<br>☐ Direct RAi<br>☐ Indirect RAi | ☐ Pure Luck<br>☐ Direct RAi<br>☐ Indirect RAi | ☐ Pure Luck<br>☐ Direct RAi<br>☐ Indirect RAi |
| **13** | **14** | **15** | **16** | **17** | **18** | **19** |
| ☐ Pure Luck<br>☐ Direct RAi<br>☐ Indirect RAi | ☐ Pure Luck<br>☐ Direct RAi<br>☐ Indirect RAi | ☐ Pure Luck<br>☐ Direct RAi<br>☐ Indirect RAi | ☐ Pure Luck<br>☐ Direct RAi<br>☐ Indirect RAi | ☐ Pure Luck<br>☐ Direct RAi<br>☐ Indirect RAi | ☐ Pure Luck<br>☐ Direct RAi<br>☐ Indirect RAi | ☐ Pure Luck<br>☐ Direct RAi<br>☐ Indirect RAi |
| **20** | **21** | **22** | **23** | **24** | **25** | **26** |
| ☐ Pure Luck<br>☐ Direct RAi<br>☐ Indirect RAi | ☐ Pure Luck<br>☐ Direct RAi<br>☐ Indirect RAi | ☐ Pure Luck<br>☐ Direct RAi<br>☐ Indirect RAi | ☐ Pure Luck<br>☐ Direct RAi<br>☐ Indirect RAi | ☐ Pure Luck<br>☐ Direct RAi<br>☐ Indirect RAi | ☐ Pure Luck<br>☐ Direct RAi<br>☐ Indirect RAi | ☐ Pure Luck<br>☐ Direct RAi<br>☐ Indirect RAi |
| **27** | **28** | **29** | **30** | **31** | | |
| ☐ Pure Luck<br>☐ Direct RAi<br>☐ Indirect RAi | ☐ Pure Luck<br>☐ Direct RAi<br>☐ Indirect RAi | ☐ Pure Luck<br>☐ Direct RAi<br>☐ Indirect RAi | ☐ Pure Luck<br>☐ Direct RAi<br>☐ Indirect RAi | ☐ Pure Luck<br>☐ Direct RAi<br>☐ Indirect RAi | ☐ Pure Luck<br>☐ Direct RAi<br>☐ Indirect RAi | ☐ Pure Luck<br>☐ Direct RAi<br>☐ Indirect RAi |

# Parenting Snakes and Ladders Calendar

**First Move.**

You need RAi. There are three ways to get it.

- Luck—You happen to be in the right place at the right time with the right mix of attributes (looks, intelligence, vulnerability, money, availability) to collect a blast of RAi from the universe and the people in it. Your survival instinct is constantly on the lookout for these opportunities (and threats). That's what happened when Emily first joined her antenatal class. She appeared to be the most knowledgeable about diet, delivery, and diapers. She was the mother most likely to succeed.
- Indirectly—You generate RAi by LOVEing others. (You hope, but had better not expect, that you will get some RAi in return. Demandingness is certain to dry up any source of RAi.) LOVEing others means noticing and making time for them, accepting and tolerating their shortcomings, and valuing them with something that you believe is important to them.
- Directly—You generate RAi by LOVEing yourself. You notice and make time for yourself, you accept and forgive your shortcomings, and you value yourself with something that is important to you.

**Second Move.**

You need RAi. There are three ways to get it.

**Third Move.**

You need RAi. There are three ways to get it.

By now you can see that repetition is required to play *Parenting Snakes and Ladders*. If you don't deliberately create RAi each day, you stop moving. You can only be happy if you are moving. Below you will see an example of a *Snakes and Ladders* calendar that you could use to establish a habit of generating RAi.

Each day has three boxes representing the three ways of experiencing RAi. Tick any box if it applies to your day. You only need to tick one box to enable you to move. If you have qualified to move, put a big cross (or tick) on the day.

## Landing on a Ladder.

This will happen when something *good* happens in the Luck box or in the Indirect box. You may have planned for it, but you really never know it will happen until it does. When it happens, your RAi has a burst of intensity, and you feel great. If you RAi level hits the Happiness Zone, you will be happy. You have definitely qualified to make your next move, but once again, you don't know if your happiness will last, and you don't have expectations one way or the other.

## Landing on a Snake.

This will happen when something *bad* happens in the Luck box or Indirect box. You might have worried about it happening in advance, but you never really know it will happen until it does. When it happens, you don't slide backwards in your progress; your progress just stops. Your RAi disappears, your frustration rises, and you feel bad. If you feel bad enough, your frustration may hit the More-on Zone and create collateral damage to yourself or others that further undermines your RAi.

Until you can restore your RAi, you are stuck. You are not qualified to make a move. This is the time to put your attention on your Direct box and generate RAi for yourself. Remember, you do that by LOVEing yourself, by using the strategy of cPR.

Filling out your calendar each day takes your focus off being stuck and creates a habit of moving forward. If you are moving, you will be satisfied, content, and even happy (if RAi is high enough to enter your Happiness Zone). Your good feelings will last as long as you keep moving.

# Parenting Snakes and Ladders Calendar

## August

| | | | | | | |
|---|---|---|---|---|---|---|
| ☐ Pure Luck<br>☐ Direct RAi<br>☐ Indirect RAi | ☐ Pure Luck<br>☐ Direct RAi<br>☐ Indirect RAi | ☐ Pure Luck<br>☐ Direct RAi<br>☐ Indirect RAi | ☐ Pure Luck<br>☐ Direct RAi<br>☐ Indirect RAi | ☐ Pure Luck<br>☐ Direct RAi<br>☐ Indirect RAi | ☐ Pure Luck<br>☐ Direct RAi<br>☐ Indirect RAi | ☐ Pure Luck<br>☐ Direct RAi<br>☐ Indirect RAi |
| **6** | **7** | **8** | **9** | **10** | **11** | **12** |
| ☐ Pure Luck<br>☐ Direct RAi<br>☐ Indirect RAi | ☐ Pure Luck<br>☐ Direct RAi<br>☐ Indirect RAi | ☐ Pure Luck<br>☐ Direct RAi<br>☐ Indirect RAi | ☐ Pure Luck<br>☐ Direct RAi<br>☐ Indirect RAi | ☐ Pure Luck<br>☐ Direct RAi<br>☐ Indirect RAi | ☐ Pure Luck<br>☐ Direct RAi<br>☐ Indirect RAi | ☐ Pure Luck<br>☐ Direct RAi<br>☐ Indirect RAi |
| **13** | **14** | **15** | **16** | **17** | **18** | **19** |
| ☐ Pure Luck<br>☐ Direct RAi<br>☐ Indirect RAi | ☐ Pure Luck<br>☐ Direct RAi<br>☐ Indirect RAi | ☐ Pure Luck<br>☐ Direct RAi<br>☐ Indirect RAi | ☐ Pure Luck<br>☐ Direct RAi<br>☐ Indirect RAi | ☐ Pure Luck<br>☐ Direct RAi<br>☐ Indirect RAi | ☐ Pure Luck<br>☐ Direct RAi<br>☐ Indirect RAi | ☐ Pure Luck<br>☐ Direct RAi<br>☐ Indirect RAi |
| **20** | **21** | **22** | **23** | **24** | **25** | **26** |
| ☐ Pure Luck<br>☐ Direct RAi<br>☐ Indirect RAi | ☐ Pure Luck<br>☐ Direct RAi<br>☐ Indirect RAi | ☐ Pure Luck<br>☐ Direct RAi<br>☐ Indirect RAi | ☐ Pure Luck<br>☐ Direct RAi<br>☐ Indirect RAi | ☐ Pure Luck<br>☐ Direct RAi<br>☐ Indirect RAi | ☐ Pure Luck<br>☐ Direct RAi<br>☐ Indirect RAi | ☐ Pure Luck<br>☐ Direct RAi<br>☐ Indirect RAi |
| **27** | **28** | **29** | **30** | **31** | | |
| ☐ Pure Luck<br>☐ Direct RAi<br>☐ Indirect RAi | ☐ Pure Luck<br>☐ Direct RAi<br>☐ Indirect RAi | ☐ Pure Luck<br>☐ Direct RAi<br>☐ Indirect RAi | ☐ Pure Luck<br>☐ Direct RAi<br>☐ Indirect RAi | ☐ Pure Luck<br>☐ Direct RAi<br>☐ Indirect RAi | ☐ Pure Luck<br>☐ Direct RAi<br>☐ Indirect RAi | ☐ Pure Luck<br>☐ Direct RAi<br>☐ Indirect RAi |

# Parenting Snakes and Ladders Calendar

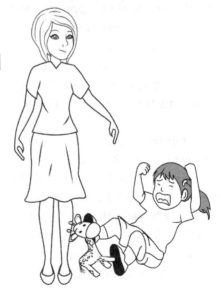

# CHAPTER 10
# WORK AND COMPETITION

Jake is so over his dad Nick calling him a Millennial. When did his dad get so smart? Jake had to look up what a Millennial was to find out what he was being accused of. If he believes his dad, Jake is a member of Generation Me—he supposedly has a disconnect between a desire for nice things and a willingness to work for them.

Politely speaking, that is so BS. Jake is not afraid of hard work. He just wants recognition, approval, and reward for doing it. But that isn't happening at work, and come to think of it, it isn't happening at home either. Jake mows the lawn, but does he get any kudos for doing so? Nope, all he gets is Nick complaining he didn't do it three weekends ago when Jake said he would. How did Jake know that the surf would be so awesome that weekend? Nick got to surf. Why shouldn't he?

Jake did well at university despite his mom getting on his back about not studying enough. He did well enough to get distinctions in most of his subjects. Combining the smarts he got from his mom and the charm he got from his dad, he succeeded in getting a job at his first interview. But he is not "feeling the love" at his accounting firm. He gets all the menial bookwork, though he is better than his boss on the accounting program the firm uses. He also gets the coffees and even sometimes is sent out to get lunch if his boss is struggling to meet a deadline.

Jake feels that he does all the hard yards (boring, repetitive, menial jobs) at work gets and gets no appreciation for it. To top it all off, at his probationary performance review, his boss told him that his attitude needs to improve. Then when his boss asked what Jake's expectations of the firm were and Jake told him he wanted a raise, his boss told him that he had to earn it. Apparently the firm is not "feeling the love" from him. It does not consider him worthy or deserving of a raise.

The relationship between Jake and his work is clearly suffering from a lack of RAi. In spite of his complaints, Jake quite likes his work, and Nick taught him never to be a quitter. If he wants to be able to hang in long enough to get RAi from his boss, Jake will need to work on improving how he feels at work.

Remember the Chicken Little story? When things happen in work situations that your instinct deems to be of life-and-death importance, you will experience negative physical reactions that promote unconscious and then conscious catastrophizing. Unless you expose your "shoulds" and reality test them, your instinct can lead to the very outcomes that you were not expecting—in this case not being appreciated and not succeeding in the firm.

Work provides an opportunity for meaning and purpose in life. It also presents an opportunity to earn an income, recognition, approval, and relative importance. Although these are necessary for survival, we don't need to get them all at work to be happy. If we are financially secure, we can be happy at work regardless of the size of our income or even if we are volunteering and not being paid at all.

However, we cannot be happy and productive at work if we lack recognition, approval, and relative importance. We don't need to be happy all of the time to be productive at work. As long as RAi is regular enough, we will work to get it and keep it. If RAi is seen to be unlikely or not possible, we might still work for the money, but our heart won't be in it, we won't show initiative, our productivity will be low, and our dissatisfaction will be high.

Because of its survival significance, conditions at work are seen by our instinct as having the potential to be especially threatening and distressing. People are often unhappy at work for reasons that have more to do with RAi than with income. Although a low income causes dissatisfaction, the buying power of income is not the only cause. The significance of income is that it is seen by people in general to be a measure of worth and therefore of RAi. If the boss earns an income many times the size of yours, comparisonitis makes sure that you feel your value to the organization is assessed to be many times less. Whether there is evidence for this is not the point. The point is that if you are frustrated and dissatisfied with your assessed worth to the organization, you will not feel respected, and you will rarely feel happy at work.

The circumstances that you experience at work are dependent on 84,000 reasons, including global economic factors, wars, terrorism, the greenhouse effect, the abuse of child workers in third-world countries, the political climate in your country, the management style of the people above you in the hierarchy, the last share dividend your organization paid its shareholders, the extent to which your managers and co-workers were bullied at school, illness experienced by your managers or co-workers, the traffic jams on the way to work, the tall poppy syndrome, the alignment of the planets, the time of the next full moon, and the beating wings of butterflies in China or Chile or Tasmania.

Since beauty is in the eye of the beholder, the way you think you are being treated at work has an even greater ability to trigger a survival reaction than any of these 84,000 reasons. If your instinct decides that you are overlooked, not validated, taken for granted, taken advantage of, being criticized, being bullied, or being ostracized, then you will start to stew. Indeed, your stewing would be much more likely and intense if you were treated like a child or a teenager.

Comparisonitis creates feelings of anxiety, anger, and despondency, and these feelings will bias your conscious thinking into more anxious, angry, and depressing thoughts. Your frustration will generate intense feelings of agitation and arousal, made all the worse by your perception that you receive no RAi at work and have no way of addressing the catastrophe that your instinct is experiencing. Your instinct might have decided that the sky is falling at work, that it does every day, and that there is absolutely nothing you can do about it if you want to keep your job.

If you want to be happy more of the time at work, you need to reduce the impact of your frustration and increase your satisfaction at work. In many ways, you have been persuaded by Western culture to think that you can do this by controlling some of the 84,000 reasons mentioned above. The reality is, our ability to change any of these in a meaningful way is extremely limited. If you put too much effort into attempting to change what you cannot, you will add to your frustration and dissatisfaction at work. The way to be happy more of the time at work is to focus more of your effort on yourself.

Frustration and satisfaction at work are tied to being noticed, being approved of, and being valued. Respect must be earned, but it also needs to be given. You can't receive it if it isn't given. There are many reasons why you might not get respect at work no matter how hard you work to earn it. If you want to be happy more often at work, you will have to generate it by focusing on what you can do for yourself instead of focusing on what work can do for you. You will need to work on yourself when you aren't getting enough RAi. It is possible to be satisfied at work even if you are the only source of RAi.

For any effort to feel worthwhile, the satisfaction you get from the effort must outweigh the frustration of making the effort. To improve the quality of your life at work, you need to better tolerate frustration and reduce its impact while at the same time create more satisfaction.

**Rubber Meets the Road.**

To increase your satisfaction and happiness at work:

- Start by getting clear about what you want to achieve. You might want to be the boss, get a good income, and get good holiday and sick pay. You might want to learn, build your experience, and step on to your next job. However, unless you feel RAi along the way, your work will become increasingly stressful. You might be able to stand it for a time, but this stress is going to cost you physically and emotionally and negatively impact the people

141

whom you love. Not much LOVEing will be going on because of the collateral damage of work stress on your mood and behavior.

- Look for the unconscious "shoulds" and "should nots" that are creating your frustration and undermining your achievement of RAi.
- Reality test and replace these thoughts with a perspective that allows you to get what you want (less frustration) and restore your RAi (more satisfaction).

Frustration and diminished RAi only occur when things are not the way they should be. So, ask yourself:

- What are my frustrations about respect, approval, and importance when I am at work? Look for the "shoulds" or "should nots" creating your frustration when things don't happen the way they should?
- What are the "shoulds" or "should nots" that determine my delivery of recognition, approval, and importance to my boss, workmates, and customers?

**As a rule, try not to "should" on yourself or anyone else. The fewer the number of "shoulds" (or "should nots") in your life, the better for you and the better for others.**

Typical frustrations at work include:

- Being micromanaged, the worst of which is being reminded to do obvious things.
- Being frequently corrected.
- Being often criticized.
- Not being listened to.
- Being told not to think and just do what you are told.
- Being told to show initiative and then being criticized or not being acknowledged for the effort.
- Being bullied or being laughed at.
- Being watched and not being trusted.
- Feeling frequently anxious, angry, or depressed.

Looking beneath these frustrations, you can see the unfulfilled expectations and desire for RAi. These frustrations are about:

- Not being respected (noticed, recognized, acknowledged).
- Not being approved of.
- Not being important.

**Psychological Resuscitation.**

**Step 1 of cPR: Calming Frustration.**

While the perspective and restoration required to resuscitate happiness will be different from situation to situation, achieving small $c$, a little bit of calm, is the first and necessary step regardless of the situation. Movement and distraction are great activities for attaining small $c$; see Chapter 7 for details on getting small $c$ and to remind yourself of the risks of drug use. Jake is fairly good at little $c$. He certainly has a life outside of work with surfing and cycling and no shortage of girlfriends.

**Step 2 of cPR: Perspective on RAi.**

Jake needs to search the three dimensions of RAi to better understand his perspective of his boss and his firm. To do this, he needs to ask questions of himself.

The first question is about being noticed:

- *Am I sensitive about my acknowledgement at work?*

"I never get any thanks for going out to get the coffee or the lunches. I have done the most training on these accounting programs than anyone in the whole office, yet all I get is the menial data entry work. I could improve their reporting systems if they bothered to ask me. And when I made a suggestion to improve a report, I wasn't thanked for doing so and instead in effect was told to speak only when spoken to. Even my wise old man listens to me some of the time. He loved the way I improved the accounting in his plumbing business. My boss just assumes that because I am new, I don't know anything. What does he think I learned and got distinctions for in school?"

The second question is about approval:

- *Am I sensitive about the approval I am getting at work?*

"Despite the number of times I have stayed late (well, once or twice) at work and finished the data input so the report could be done on time, I never even got a 'thank you.' I might be only a small cog in the engine around here, but surely someone should tell me I do good work. I know I do."

The third question is about importance:

- *Am I sensitive about not being considered important at work?*

"From what I can tell, everyone got a raise after the last performance review except for me. I know my employment status was promoted from provisional to permanent, but so what? It didn't mean any more money, and to me it means my boss can continue to take advantage of me. I get the impression that he thinks I can just leave if I am unhappy. He doesn't care. I am not important to him."

You have to first bring these thoughts to the surface before you can moderate the collateral damage that they cause.

**"To learn the secrets of life, we must first become aware of them." (Albert Einstein)**

Below are examples of surfaced thoughts that, once identified, can be normalized to moderate instinct's sensitivity to perceived loss of RAi at work.

HMS Unconscious Thoughts

Work

You may identify with some of them. You don't need to find all of your instinct's comparisonitis and catastrophizing. All you need to do is to identify a small number of clear thoughts that highlight instinct's fears. The work we do with these few will generalize to all of them and prepare us to move on to restoration.

Examples:

"People will treat me unfairly at work some of the time, but it will never mean that the sky is falling. When people disrespect me at work, it is only an acorn. I want but don't need the approval of others at work to survive. I also don't expect that thinking this way will totally stop instinct from catastrophizing, but I believe it will help it settle down."

"I have to remind myself that any experience of disrespect in other areas of my life will increase instinct's insecurity and overreaction to being treated poorly at work. I need to look for the additive negative effect of past experience making what is happening at work worse. If I can do this, I will be less likely to blame only work for my bad feelings and less likely to accept instinct's view that the sky is falling."

These thoughts and responses to them need to be recognized as examples of what is happening initially at an unconscious level in the limbic system and then at a conscious level in the frontal lobe. They are examples of instinctive survival responses to situations that are not survival situations.

**Competition is a form of striving for recognition, approval, and relative importance. It is a natural expression of our survival instinct and is another way of generating RAi. In a way, we are all competitors. We compete for survival in so many ways related to work, housing, food, schooling, business, parking, queues, and safety. We are all competitors for the limited resources, limited opportunities, and limited safety in the world we live in.**

**The value of competition in satisfying our survival instinct does not come from winning. Winning is not everything! In fact, winning is such a rare outcome of competition that it is a meager source of recognition, approval, and relative importance. Winners will tell you when the grin fades that the "sparkle" of winning does not survive the interval between wins, and in reality, does not last very long at all. From your instinct's perspective, the primary sources of recognition, approval, and relative importance in competition are the opportunities for group membership (instinctive safety in numbers) and the opportunity for favorable comparisonitis (RAi) within the group.**

The satisfaction of competing does not come from winning; almost nobody wins. The reward of competition comes from identifying oneself as a competitor, from being recognized as a competitor, and from comparisonitis—comparing one's performance to oneself and others. Getting out there and sharing and comparing the effort with others is what matters. Competitors get recognition, validation, and approval every single time they get out there whether actually competing or just training. This is why competition is such a popular activity even though very few people ever win.

Sometimes, however, too much of a good thing can be a problem. Competition becomes a problem when it becomes too fatiguing, too intense, and so important that it overshadows other sources of approval and relative importance like being healthy, having good relationships, work performance, socializing, or parenting. If overused, competition gets into a pattern of providing satisfaction at the cost of dissatisfaction in other life activities and collateral damage to your relationships.

When you are competing, don't aim to win or even to do your best.

Winning depends on 84,000 variables, including many things beyond your control like the weather, the quality of the food you have been eating recently, the amount of sleep you had, and how lucky you are today. Aiming to do your best triggers comparisonitis of the past with present performance. Winning and doing your best are circumstances that you cannot control, and this knowledge is a source of worry for your survival instinct. It puts instinct in a "sky is falling" frame of mind before you even start. It creates excessive performance anxiety and burns up a lot of energy.

Instead of aiming to win or do your best, aim to compete.

> **What it means to compete will be unique to each competitor. It could mean just keeping up with the competitor next to you; or surging away to measure their current strength; sticking to your plan for every serve or going for your shots regardless of the score; continually returning your focus to your swing, your stroke, your power; trying something different just to see what happens; faking weakness to gain a surprise advantage; stressing the competitors by pushing into your pain barrier because you can. Competing could mean just getting out there, just starting, just finishing.**
>
> **When you compete, you are in total control. You have no control over the outcome of your effort, but in the heat of the moment, you are in control of what you do, and through doing, you create the opportunity for recognition, approval, and relative importance.**

If it was pointed out to him, Jake is more than capable of understanding:

- How his RAi at worked is being blocked by his reactive "shoulds" to circumstances outside of his ability to affect the 84,000 variables influencing his boss and the accounting framework the firm uses.
- How these circumstances are serious but not of life-and-death significance; they do not warrant "shoulds."
- How his instinct is relating to these circumstances as if they are life-and-death and consequently accelerating his not feeling "the love" by increasing comparisonitis and catastrophizing.

But this understanding will elude Jake (he is "shoulding" on his boss and his firm something fierce) while he remains focused on fairness and justice and reward.

### Step 3 of cPR: Restoration of RAi

Perspective on missing RAi will normalize instinct's catastrophizing and prepare you for the goal of restoration. Restoration of satisfaction and happiness when faced with work difficulties requires you to:

- Restore recognition.

- Restore approval.
- Restore importance.

Restoration requires:

- An openness for action.
- A willingness to take risks.
- A determination to learn from outcomes.
- An ability to improvise and adapt.

Dealing with unwanted circumstances can lead to such intense levels of frustration that you readily get to the point of giving up. If you get stopped by your bad feelings, you can get moving again by following the restoration routine of risk-taking and action learning.

Effective risk-taking requires you to:

- Assess the possible consequences of your actions before you take them.
- Put a value on the worthiness of the risk.
- Work up the courage to take the risk.
- Have in place strategies to tolerate the anxiety associated with the proposed risk.

A method of measuring the value of a risk is to estimate the balance between the anxiety of taking the risk (the downside) and the future satisfaction from taking the risk (the upside). If you are likely to be satisfied with the future consequences of your action and you can tolerate the frustration, it's worth taking. If you are likely to be dissatisfied with future consequences, then it's not worth taking. Even if you are satisfied now, you need to think about future satisfaction. Satisfaction today is not worth dissatisfaction tomorrow.

You don't require a crystal ball to evaluate risks. All you need do is take some time and think about possible future consequences. You don't require a crystal ball to evaluate risks. All you need do is take some time and think about possible future consequences. Action learning requires a definition of success and a means of objective measurement of progress. It requires a focus on developing the skills needed for development, on motivation to practice these skills, and openness to keep adapting effort in the face of objective evidence.

The restoration ideas and strategies that you plan and put into action only need a possibility of success. You are not going to come up with a plan that guarantees minimum frustration, satisfaction, confidence, and happiness because 84,000 things in your environment will continue to affect the outcome. This means that no matter how carefully you plan for an outcome, something may still go wrong.

**Love is the default restoration strategy.**

Using this strategy at work will be a little different than using it in intimate relationships or using it in parenting.

**L**—for active listening at work means hearing and talking to yourself when you pick up on taking something personally. When you start thinking that whatever is happening is "all about me" rather than "partly about me and partly about my boss," you are actively listening to your own instinctive sensitivity catastrophizing about the terribleness of whatever just happened.

**O**—for overlooking at work requires effort to reduce or at least mask the disapproval you show your boss or bosses over their treatment of you. Reducing the disapproval that you show your bosses over the things they do that trigger your survival instinct can significantly improve their sense of your acceptance and approval. To do this, you need to consciously remind yourself that things are mostly not life-and-death. This reality test helps you tolerate instinct's conclusion that your bosses' continued doing of things that you feel demean you are a catastrophe and reflect on your bosses' stuff rather than on you.

**V**—stands for valuing. When you do things that your boss has asked for, things that are important to your boss, your boss feels valued. Once you realize that what is important to your boss will change over time and will be inconsistent, you are in the position to consistently value your boss and preserve their sense of relative importance. To adequately appreciate your boss, you need to listen and observe with active reflection. At work, you do this with action more than with words. Don't get into a "deep and meaningful" with your boss. Show you have listened with what you do. You don't have to respect the boss; you can respect the position.

**E**—stands for effort, consistency of effort. If you love to surf, you will do it often, and your skill will grow. You can never be certain that persistently making an effort at work will be noticed, but you can be certain that not making an effort will be. You nurture relative importance at work by showing the love on a regular basis.

If this doesn't indirectly generate RAi from your boss, it will generate RAi from yourself.

The following thoughts are examples of restoration ideas. For them to be useful, action has to follow.

"I just keep going over and over and over how badly I am treated at work. I'm not getting anywhere, and I can't stop! Stewing is normal. As long as it is in my head, I might as well work with it and help Ducky come up with a plan of action for next time. I can turn what I should have said last time into what I plan to say next time. I can turn what I should have done into what I plan to do. I can evaluate any plan for future action by guessing about what would likely happen and how I would handle that."

"I remember that when it comes to influencing other people, their instinctive survival fears control their attention and approval. If I want more attention, validation, and approval at work, my efforts can be directed at influencing their concerns for survival. I remember that the blueprint for all survival patterns is 'if I am noticed, approved of, and relatively important, I am safe.' So, my plan is to continue as best I can to provide RAi for myself and to notice, validate, and approve of people at work."

From your instinct's perspective, the risk of taking action to improve your satisfaction at work is that your efforts might fail, it might get worse, and this will undermine relative importance in your own eyes, or in the eyes of your family or friends. Your instinct wants you to believe that if your relative importance worsens, you will not and cannot survive, and that's the worst thing that can happen. When you are calm, these conclusions are clearly irrational. When you are upset, they feel real.

**Summary.**

**Having satisfying experiences at work requires:**

- **A clear picture of what it will take to satisfy your instinct's survival fears in your work environment. You need a clear idea of what it would take to feel noticed, approved of, and important at work and a clear understanding of how to get it. Having a clear intention and plan of action allows your effort in feeling happy at work to be both strategic and reactive.**
- **Reactive behavior at work is based on your ability to release the pressure of your frustration when things are dissatisfying and on your determination to see the behavior of people at work to be caused by their instinctive fears and not as evidence of their character or how they feel about you. It is more useful to think that people at work approve of you at least some of the time, and when they can't show it, it is because they are going through their own "sky is falling" moment with their insecurity and fear.**
- **Strategic behavior at work is driven by the general strategy that you satisfy your instinct's need for RAi directly as well as indirectly from others. Other people at work seek RAi like you do. Part of your strategy is to discover through risk-taking and action learning what is required to increase others' sense of recognition, approval, and relative importance and to make it happen.**
- **Effective strategy sees survival fear as normal and requires you to become skilled in your ability to tolerate the anxiety associated with it. Seek temporary relief from it, but don't put any energy into eliminating it. It won't go away.**
- **Starting the game of *Work Snakes and Ladders*.**

**Establishing a Habit.**

If you haven't read about *Snakes and Ladders* as a game of life in Chapter 8, take a look now. It's at the end of the chapter.

**Work Snakes and Ladders**

# Work Snakes  and Ladders Calendar

## August

| | | 1 | 2 | 3 | 4 | 5 |
|---|---|---|---|---|---|---|
| ☐ Pure Luck<br>☐ Direct RAi<br>☐ Indirect RAi | ☐ Pure Luck<br>☐ Direct RAi<br>☐ Indirect RAi | ☐ Pure Luck<br>☐ Direct RAi<br>☐ Indirect RAi | ☐ Pure Luck<br>☐ Direct RAi<br>☐ Indirect RAi | ☐ Pure Luck<br>☐ Direct RAi<br>☐ Indirect RAi | ☐ Pure Luck<br>☐ Direct RAi<br>☐ Indirect RAi | ☐ Pure Luck<br>☐ Direct RAi<br>☐ Indirect RAi |
| 6 | 7 | 8 | 9 | 10 | 11 | 12 |
| ☐ Pure Luck<br>☐ Direct RAi<br>☐ Indirect RAi | ☐ Pure Luck<br>☐ Direct RAi<br>☐ Indirect RAi | ☐ Pure Luck<br>☐ Direct RAi<br>☐ Indirect RAi | ☐ Pure Luck<br>☐ Direct RAi<br>☐ Indirect RAi | ☐ Pure Luck<br>☐ Direct RAi<br>☐ Indirect RAi | ☐ Pure Luck<br>☐ Direct RAi<br>☐ Indirect RAi | ☐ Pure Luck<br>☐ Direct RAi<br>☐ Indirect RAi |
| 13 | 14 | 15 | 16 | 17 | 18 | 19 |
| ☐ Pure Luck<br>☐ Direct RAi<br>☐ Indirect RAi | ☐ Pure Luck<br>☐ Direct RAi<br>☐ Indirect RAi | ☐ Pure Luck<br>☐ Direct RAi<br>☐ Indirect RAi | ☐ Pure Luck<br>☐ Direct RAi<br>☐ Indirect RAi | ☐ Pure Luck<br>☐ Direct RAi<br>☐ Indirect RAi | ☐ Pure Luck<br>☐ Direct RAi<br>☐ Indirect RAi | ☐ Pure Luck<br>☐ Direct RAi<br>☐ Indirect RAi |
| 20 | 21 | 22 | 23 | 24 | 25 | 26 |
| ☐ Pure Luck<br>☐ Direct RAi<br>☐ Indirect RAi | ☐ Pure Luck<br>☐ Direct RAi<br>☐ Indirect RAi | ☐ Pure Luck<br>☐ Direct RAi<br>☐ Indirect RAi | ☐ Pure Luck<br>☐ Direct RAi<br>☐ Indirect RAi | ☐ Pure Luck<br>☐ Direct RAi<br>☐ Indirect RAi | ☐ Pure Luck<br>☐ Direct RAi<br>☐ Indirect RAi | ☐ Pure Luck<br>☐ Direct RAi<br>☐ Indirect RAi |
| 27 | 28 | 29 | 30 | 31 | | |
| ☐ Pure Luck<br>☐ Direct RAi<br>☐ Indirect RAi | ☐ Pure Luck<br>☐ Direct RAi<br>☐ Indirect RAi | ☐ Pure Luck<br>☐ Direct RAi<br>☐ Indirect RAi | ☐ Pure Luck<br>☐ Direct RAi<br>☐ Indirect RAi | ☐ Pure Luck<br>☐ Direct RAi<br>☐ Indirect RAi | ☐ Pure Luck<br>☐ Direct RAi<br>☐ Indirect RAi | ☐ Pure Luck<br>☐ Direct RAi<br>☐ Indirect RAi |

Work Snakes and Ladders
Calendar

**First Move.**

You need RAi. There are three ways to get it.

- Luck—You happen to be in the right place at the right time with the right mix of attributes (looks, intelligence, vulnerability, money, availability) to collect a blast of RAi from the universe and the people in it. Your survival instinct is constantly on the lookout for these opportunities (and threats).
- Indirectly—You generate RAi by LOVEing others. (You hope, but had better not expect, that you will get some RAi in return. Demandingness is certain to dry up any source of RAi.) LOVEing others means noticing and making time for them, accepting and tolerating their shortcomings, and valuing them with something that you believe is important to them.
- Directly—You generate RAi by LOVEing yourself. You notice and make time for yourself, you accept and forgive your shortcomings, and you value yourself with something that is important to you.

**Second Move.**

You need RAi. There are three ways to get it.

**Third Move.**

You need RAi. There are three ways to get it.

By now you can see that repetition is required to play *Snakes and Ladders*. If you don't deliberately create RAi each day, you stop moving. You can only be happy if you are moving. Below you will see an example of a *Snakes and Ladders* calendar that you could use to establish a habit of generating RAi.

Each day has three boxes representing the three ways of experiencing RAi. Tick any box if it applies to your day. You only need to tick one box to enable you to move. If you have qualified to move, put a big cross (or tick) on the day.

**Landing on a Ladder.**

This will happen when something *good* happens in the Luck box or in the Indirect box. You may have planned for it, but you really never know it will happen until it does. When it happens, your RAi has a burst of intensity, and you feel great. If you RAi level hits the Happiness Zone, you will be happy. You have definitely qualified to make your next move, but once again, you don't know if your happiness will last, and you don't have expectations one way or the other.

**Landing on a Snake.**

This will happen when something *bad* happens in the Luck box or Indirect box. You might have worried about it happening in advance, but you never really know it will happen until it does. When it happens, you don't slide backwards in your progress; your progress just stops. Your RAi disappears, your frustration rises, and you feel bad. If you feel bad enough, your frustration may hit the More-on Zone and create collateral damage to yourself or others that further undermines your RAi.

Until you can restore your RAi, you are stuck. You are not qualified to make a move. This is the time to put your attention on your Direct box and generate RAi for yourself. Remember, you do that by LOVEing yourself, by using the strategy of cPR.

Filling out your calendar each day takes your focus off being stuck and creates a habit of moving forward. If you are moving, you will be satisfied, content, and even happy (if RAi is high enough to enter your Happiness Zone). Your good feelings will last as long as you keep moving.

# Work Snakes  and Ladders Calendar
## August

| | | 1 | 2 | 3 | 4 | 5 |
|---|---|---|---|---|---|---|
| ☐ Pure Luck<br>☐ Direct RAi<br>☐ Indirect RAi | ☐ Pure Luck<br>☐ Direct RAi<br>☐ Indirect RAi | ☐ Pure Luck<br>☐ Direct RAi<br>☐ Indirect RAi | ☐ Pure Luck<br>☐ Direct RAi<br>☐ Indirect RAi | ☐ Pure Luck<br>☐ Direct RAi<br>☐ Indirect RAi | ☐ Pure Luck<br>☐ Direct RAi<br>☐ Indirect RAi | ☐ Pure Luck<br>☐ Direct RAi<br>☐ Indirect RAi |
| 6 | 7 | 8 | 9 | 10 | 11 | 12 |
| ☐ Pure Luck<br>☐ Direct RAi<br>☐ Indirect RAi | ☐ Pure Luck<br>☐ Direct RAi<br>☐ Indirect RAi | ☐ Pure Luck<br>☐ Direct RAi<br>☐ Indirect RAi | ☐ Pure Luck<br>☐ Direct RAi<br>☐ Indirect RAi | ☐ Pure Luck<br>☐ Direct RAi<br>☐ Indirect RAi | ☐ Pure Luck<br>☐ Direct RAi<br>☐ Indirect RAi | ☐ Pure Luck<br>☐ Direct RAi<br>☐ Indirect RAi |
| 13 | 14 | 15 | 16 | 17 | 18 | 19 |
| ☐ Pure Luck<br>☐ Direct RAi<br>☐ Indirect RAi | ☐ Pure Luck<br>☐ Direct RAi<br>☐ Indirect RAi | ☐ Pure Luck<br>☐ Direct RAi<br>☐ Indirect RAi | ☐ Pure Luck<br>☐ Direct RAi<br>☐ Indirect RAi | ☐ Pure Luck<br>☐ Direct RAi<br>☐ Indirect RAi | ☐ Pure Luck<br>☐ Direct RAi<br>☐ Indirect RAi | ☐ Pure Luck<br>☐ Direct RAi<br>☐ Indirect RAi |
| 20 | 21 | 22 | 23 | 24 | 25 | 26 |
| ☐ Pure Luck<br>☐ Direct RAi<br>☐ Indirect RAi | ☐ Pure Luck<br>☐ Direct RAi<br>☐ Indirect RAi | ☐ Pure Luck<br>☐ Direct RAi<br>☐ Indirect RAi | ☐ Pure Luck<br>☐ Direct RAi<br>☐ Indirect RAi | ☐ Pure Luck<br>☐ Direct RAi<br>☐ Indirect RAi | ☐ Pure Luck<br>☐ Direct RAi<br>☐ Indirect RAi | ☐ Pure Luck<br>☐ Direct RAi<br>☐ Indirect RAi |
| 27 | 28 | 29 | 30 | 31 | | |
| ☐ Pure Luck<br>☐ Direct RAi<br>☐ Indirect RAi | ☐ Pure Luck<br>☐ Direct RAi<br>☐ Indirect RAi | ☐ Pure Luck<br>☐ Direct RAi<br>☐ Indirect RAi | ☐ Pure Luck<br>☐ Direct RAi<br>☐ Indirect RAi | ☐ Pure Luck<br>☐ Direct RAi<br>☐ Indirect RAi | ☐ Pure Luck<br>☐ Direct RAi<br>☐ Indirect RAi | ☐ Pure Luck<br>☐ Direct RAi<br>☐ Indirect RAi |

Work Snakes and Ladders
Calendar

# CHAPTER 11
# BUREAUCRACY

Emily has been a customer for over thirteen years. Now that Jake has gone out on his own, and Abbey is hardly ever home, the shows that she and Nick watch on TV have changed quite significantly. She is trying to negotiate a change to her subscription involving the removal of one of the two connection boxes she has in the house. She also wants to drop her subscription to movies and replace it with a subscription to TV series, while at the same time keeping access to documentaries. It has now been almost forty-five minutes, and she has been transferred twice. The girl said she had to talk to her supervisor and would be right back. That was over five minutes ago.

Apparently, there is a problem with the boxes and with the program changes she is asking for. When she rang last week, she was told then that it couldn't be done. After Emily hung up the phone and thought about it, that didn't make sense, so she rang again today. The first girl that answered also told her that it couldn't be done. Emily was determined and replied by saying she would cancel her subscription. That got some reaction. The girl went away and came back and said that it could be done. After a flash of satisfaction, Emily asked what the new monthly rate would be. She was told that it would be the same.

Emily was not impressed. Emily was a university graduate. She had worked as a solicitor for ten years after her kids reached high school, so she was no intellectual slouch. But the answer she got made no sense at all. It was something having to do with her subscription to two boxes, one supercharged and one standard. The one she wanted to give back was the supercharged one, and she wanted to keep the standard one. Well the company didn't support the non-supercharged ones anymore, so she couldn't give back the supercharged one and therefore couldn't save any money on her subscription. In addition to that, she couldn't have access to the documentaries if she didn't subscribe to the movies, so if she wanted to keep the documentaries and have access to TV series, she had to pay extra.

Emily dug her heels in and told the girl that it was all too hard and that she would just cancel her subscription. This sent the girl back to her supervisor. Emily was still waiting. The girl came back and said that she was sorry, but Emily would have to keep the supercharged box and pay more for the TV series. Emily took a breath, she had been afraid the girl would say that and was wondering if she and Nick could survive without their documentaries. But Emily stepped out anyway. She told the girl she wanted to cancel her subscription of thirteen years and was put on hold again while she was transferred to the cancellation department.

Emily managed her frustration and fear of doing the wrong thing a little longer while she waited and then went through the cancellation process. Done and dusted, she went to cook dinner. Cooking was relaxing for her, especially now that she only cooked for herself and Nick. And she enjoyed a glass of wine while she cooked.

The next day, she received a call from the media company saying that they didn't want to lose her as a customer. She was told that somehow she had been transferred to the wrong department yesterday and was given the wrong information. She could have all that she wanted and save fifteen dollars a month. However, in that twenty-four-hour period, Emily had calmed down enough to realize that of course she and Nick could survive without the documentaries; they could get them from other sources if they needed to.

Emily was on a new path to reduce the frustration in her life, and for her, dumping her media company was a step along the way.

When things happen in your dealings with bureaucracy that your instinct deems to be of life-and-death importance, you will experience increasingly negative physical reactions that promote unconscious and then conscious catastrophizing. Unless you expose your "shoulds" and reality test them, your instinct can lead to the very outcome that you were not wanting—in this case, feeling so powerless that you give up and give in and dislike yourself for weakness afterwards.

Most if not all bureaucracies use excessively complicated administrative procedures and acronyms like ECAPs (Excessively Complicated Administrative Procedures) to make them difficult to understand. It seems like our worst and most common frustrations come from having to deal with service bureaucracies. Yes, they are the ones that are supposed to make our lives safer, easier, and more satisfying.

Government agencies, power companies, banks, insurance companies, telephone companies, internet service providers, and digital entertainment providers are good examples of bureaucracies where we inwardly groan whenever we have to deal with them. If it's a service that you need or one that you have contracted, you can't go anywhere else. If it's a service you want but don't need, you are important and will be treated well at first—that is until you sign and pay. You might think that once you have become a client or customer, your relative importance to the bureaucracy has increased, and you can expect special treatment. However, in most cases, the reverse is true. From the moment that you sign up, your importance becomes less than everybody who hasn't signed up or paid. As an existing customer, you don't get access to all the goodies that are offered to entice new customers. Why offer them to you? You already are a customer, and they have your money. Keeping your business is not as important as getting new business. As soon as your status moves from new to existing, it seems that bureaucracies make it difficult for you to communicate with them. This difficulty creates massive amounts of frustration and catastrophizing.

Does all this sound a bit negative? Well, it is what it is. If you haven't had the experience of wanting to reach through the phone and shake somebody, you haven't lived long enough. Eventually you will sign up for something and, bingo, another casualty of excessively complicated administrative procedures.

Bureaucracies and their customers have the same instinctive need to survive. The problem is that bureaucracies pursue key performance indicators like income targets and budgeted expenditures to survive, and customers pursue RAi to survive. It seems entirely sensible that treating customers well and providing a quality service would lead to them feel relatively important and guarantee their loyalty and repeat business. However, when bureaucracy's survival is at stake, comparisonitis and catastrophizing cause a fog of instinct that nullifies their logic and common sense. When bureaucracies catastrophize, they focus on growing income through new business and on cutting costs by reducing service. The strategies they use to pursue these goals prioritize new clients and erode the quality of service to existing customers. Under pressure, the question bureaucracies obsess about is "How can we make more and spend less?" When relative importance and survival are measured so differently, it is rare for both the provider and customer to win. Since bureaucracies have the power, they almost always win, and the customer, being virtually powerless, almost always loses.

In summary, the ECAPs (excessively complicated administrative procedures) that bureaucracies use and the frustration and unhappiness they cause are a natural and inevitable consequence of comparisonitis and catastrophizing. In bureaucracies, comparisonitis shows itself as a compulsion to compare income and expenditure budgets from one moment to the next to determine relative success. Although comparisonitis occasionally highlights improvements, it is more concerned with things going wrong than with things going right and doesn't allow for dwelling on positives too long. Success doesn't threaten survival, but a lack of success does. When comparisonitis shows a setback, bureaucracies catastrophize and put new ECAPs in place to increase income and reduce expenditures. They increase revenue by focusing on new clients and services, and cut their running costs by cutting the quality of service to existing customers and clients.

How do they get away with this? Well, that's where ECAPs come in. By using excessively complicated administrative procedures, institutions make external scrutiny very challenging. ECAPs provide escape clauses that excuse not providing the service or assistance that you expect to receive. They hide these "escapes clauses" in very small print buried in massive "Terms and Conditions" documents that hardly anyone—except the people who wrote them—ever read. Particularly important, ECAPs are used to frustrate you enough to make you give up seeking a fair go. Or they are used to push you into the More-on Zone and then blame your behavior for their treatment of you. Has anyone noticed the increasing number of signs like this at service centers?

"Abusive language will not be tolerated."

ECAPs are the hammer and we, the customers, are the nail.

For any effort to feel worthwhile, the satisfaction you get from the effort has to outweigh the frustration of making an effort. To deal with bureaucracy more effectively, you need to work on tolerating the frustration, reducing the impact of frustration, and on increasing your satisfaction

**Rubber Meets the Road.**

To increase your confidence and satisfaction in dealing with bureaucracy:

- Start by getting clear about what you want to achieve. Wanting fairness is vague; wanting a refund is clear. Wanting them to provide you what they promised is vague; wanting a working internet connection is clear.
- Look for the unconscious "shoulds" and "should nots" that are creating your frustration and undermining your RAi.
- Reality test and replace these thoughts with a perspective that allows you to seek what you want with less frustration and restore your RAi regardless of the actual outcome.

Frustration and diminished RAi only occur when things are not the way they should be. So, ask yourself:

- What are my frustrations with the service I am getting? Look for the "shoulds" or "should nots" creating your frustration when things don't happen the way they should.
- What are the "shoulds" or "should nots" that determine my recognition, approval, and importance as a customer?

**As a rule, try not to "should" on yourself or anyone else. The fewer the number of "shoulds" (or "should nots") in your life, the better for you and the better for others.**

Typical frustrations with bureaucracy include waiting time in queues; voice recognition software that does not work; call center staff that cannot be understood; call center computers not working; being put on hold; being transferred; being given conflicting information; being given explanations that do not make sense; feeling rushed.

Typical dissatisfactions include seeing offers made to entice new customers that don't apply to existing customers; not receiving any service; not receiving a quality service; being locked into a one-size-fits-all mentality; being treated as a number rather than as a person; having next to no influence on outcomes.

These frustrations and dissatisfactions reflect underlying "shoulds" and "should nots."

- "I shouldn't have to wait this long."
- "Call center staff should speak my language or have accents that I can understand."
- "Someone should be able to give me a straight answer."
- "They don't care about my time, and they should."
- "They think that 'We are experiencing a particularly busy period right now. Please call back later' is OK. Too bad. Suck it up. You have no choice."
- "They don't listen, and they should."
- "They act like they have all the power. I am the one who pays, so I should have the power."

Regarding your perspective on "shoulds," circumstances may or may not have happened the way you see them. Whether something happened the way you see it is not important. What matters is that you think something happened. Beauty is in the eye of the beholder and so is fact, truth, and reality. You are going to work to increase your satisfaction primarily by changing the eye of the beholder (your perspective), then your behavior, and maybe (remote chance) the behavior of the bureaucracy.

In an attempt to get more RAi from looking at past situations differently, or from planning the perfect response in a future situation, you might be focusing on how you could change the perspective and behavior of the bureaucracy. However, it is next to impossible to come up with a plan that will consistently get RAi from bureaucracy. The difficulty of manipulating or coercing bureaucracy in pursuit of RAi lies in the 84,000 variables affecting it that are outside of your influence. These external variables reset your importance to a bureaucracy the moment you hang up the phone. It is what it is. Don't expect it to be any different.

**Psychological Resuscitation**

**Step 1 of cPR: Calming Frustration.**

While the perspective and restoration required to resuscitate happiness will be different from situation to situation, achieving small *c*, a little bit of calm, is the first and necessary step regardless of the situation. Movement and distraction are great activities for attaining small *c*; see Chapter 7 for details on getting small *c* and to remind yourself of the risks of drug use.

**Step 2 of cPR: Perspective on RAi.**

Emily can search the three dimensions of RAi to better understand her distressing perspective of having to deal with bureaucracy. She needs to ask questions of herself.

The first question is about being seen as more than an account number.

- *Am I sensitive about bureaucracy treating me just as a number?*

"When I was getting ready to sign up for the service, bureaucracy was willing to talk to me until I was talked out, and then to keep asking me if I had further questions. Now that they have my business, they can't get rid of me fast enough, put me hold for extended periods of time, tell me to ring back when they are less busy, and expect me to know when that is. None of this should happen. It is so wrong!"

The second question is about approval:

- *Am I sensitive about the approval (reward) I get as a customer?*

"It seems I got more approval before I became a customer. Now that I am a customer, there is no approval, no reward. Sure, they offer special deals but not to existing customers. They should offer the deals to existing customers first. That way they might keep their customers longer."

The third question is about importance:

- *Am I sensitive about having any importance to the bureaucracy?*

"I clearly have no importance to the bureaucracy. Now that they have my money, they seem to care very little about the service they provide. They say they do, but their actions speak so much louder than their words. They should show they care about their customers instead of just saying that they care."

You have to first appreciate that your instinct is thinking this way to be able to moderate the collateral damage these thoughts cause.

**"To learn the secrets of life, we must first become aware of them."
Albert Einstein**

Below are examples of surfaced thoughts that, once identified, can be normalized to moderate instinct's sensitivity to perceived loss of RAi when dealing with bureaucracy.

You may identify with some of them. You don't need to find all of your instinct's comparisonitis and catastrophizing. All you need to do is to identify a small number of clear thoughts that highlight instinct's fears. The work we do with a few will generalize to all of them and prepare us to move on to restoration.

Examples:

"I understand that instinct sees the behavior of bureaucracy as disregarding my relative importance as an individual. The nonsense of its administrative procedures is clearly there for the benefit of the organization and not for me. It couldn't care less about me. Instinct believes they shouldn't treat me this way."

"Instinct sees this as a survival threat and pushes me to meekly accept the way bureaucracy treats me to avoid frustration and maintain some relative importance. But when I give in, I feel weak and unhappy about being taken advantage of. I shouldn't be so weak and give in!"

"I started to feel angry when I had to wait and wait and wait. When I did get to talk to someone, I had to explain the story repeatedly. No one seems to keep good records, and no one is interested in me. Instinct has concluded that I must be invisible, that my relative importance is small. I got angry because I was so anxious about my survival."

"Instinct's fear of powerlessness winds me up when I have to deal with bureaucracy. It believes that I should be treated well, and that it is a catastrophe when I am not. Given treatment like this in the past, instinct causes me to feel dissatisfied before the interaction has even begun."

"I understand that uninvited thoughts are a side effect of instinct working to restore my RAi. The difficulty of tolerating ECAPs naturally affects me in the form of catastrophizing thoughts—the sky is falling. Catastrophizing is the way my survival instinct pushes me into action, but this makes my bad feelings worse. Distress provides the energy to complete the process of figuring out how to improve my survival chances. Unfortunately, it also triggers a compulsion to stew even when I don't want to, or to give in and suffer the consequences of my avoidance."

"If I act differently next time, will I approve of my actions, and will the consequences of my actions be useful?"

## Step 3 of cPR: Restoration of RAi

Perspective on missing RAi will normalize instinct's catastrophizing and prepare you for the goal of restoration. Restoration of satisfaction and when dealing with bureaucracy requires you to:

- Restore recognition.
- Restore approval.
- Restore importance.

Restoration requires:

- An openness for action.
- A willingness to take risks.
- A determination to learn from outcomes.
- An ability to improvise and adapt.

Dealing with unwanted circumstances can lead to such intense levels of frustration that you readily get to the point of giving up. If you get stopped by your bad feelings, you can get moving again by following the restoration routine of risk-taking and action learning.

Effective risk-taking requires you to:

- Assess the possible consequences of your actions before you take them.
- Put a value on the worthiness of the risk.
- Work up the courage to take the risk.
- Have in place strategies to tolerate the anxiety associated with the proposed risk.

A method of measuring the value of a risk is to estimate the balance between the anxiety of taking the risk (the downside) and the future satisfaction from taking the risk (the upside). If you are likely to be satisfied with the future consequences of your action, and you can tolerate the frustration, it's worth taking. If you are likely to be dissatisfied with future consequences, then it's not worth taking. Even if you are satisfied now, you need to think about future satisfaction. Satisfaction today is not worth dissatisfaction tomorrow.

You don't require a crystal ball to evaluate risks. All you need do is take some time and think about possible future consequences. Action learning requires a definition of success and a means of objective measurement of progress. It requires a focus on acquiring the skills needed for development, the motivation to practice these skills, and the openness to keep adapting efforts in the face of objective evidence.

The restoration ideas and strategies that you plan and put into action only need a possibility of success. You are not going to come up with a plan that guarantees minimum frustration, satisfaction, confidence, and happiness, because 84,000 things in your environment will continue to affect the outcome. This means that no matter how carefully you plan for an outcome, something may still go wrong.

You can use LOVE to restore RAi when dealing with bureaucracy but only for yourself. LOVEing yourself on a phone call to one of your so-called service providers is about:

- Treating yourself to a cuppa during the call (or anything rewarding that is not related to the bureaucracy—you will have plenty of time to do this while you wait).
- Not judging yourself negatively when you want to reach through and throttle someone.
- Giving yourself a high five every time you repeat yourself.

Don't bother to use LOVE on the bureaucracy to generate RAi. It doesn't care. It can't afford to care about you, only about its budgets. It is what it is.

The restoration ideas and strategies that you plan and put into action only need a possibility of success. You are not going to come up with a plan that guarantees minimum frustration, satisfaction, confidence, and happiness because 84,000 things in your environment will continue to affect both you and bureaucracy. This means that no matter how carefully you plan for an outcome, something may still go wrong.

Objectively measuring progress in handling bureaucracy might be taking stock of bureaucratic issues that you have been avoiding and planning to reduce this number. Things that we procrastinate about or avoid include doing taxes; looking for a better mortgage rate or a better electricity supply rate; a better mobile phone plan; better insurance premiums for house and car; better medical insurance; better internet or entertainment packages. Many of us just pay yearly renewals without looking for better deals. We do this because of the frustration we feel and the whack that our RAi takes when dealing with the bureaucracies that supply these services. The money we lose doing this has been called the *lazy tax*.

The following thoughts are examples of restoration ideas. For them to be useful, action has to follow.

"I am not going to wait for yearly renewals. I am going to start now, choose one at a time, and slowly plan for what I need to do to get a better deal, and then put the plan into action. No rush is required, and I will be careful to manage the day-to-day frustration level in my tank so that I have space for the increased frustration that negotiating a better deal will generate. During the negotiation, I am going to release the pressure of my frustration and catastrophizing by counting backwards. I will then remind myself that my distress is normal, should be happening, and is a source of energy for what I am about to do."

You can never know whether you are going to feel satisfied on any occasion, but you can learn, improvise, and adapt. Increase the frequency of activities that seem to produce RAi and get the odds of increased satisfaction and potential happiness in your favor.

An essential element of restoration is to include self-talk that motivates action and a strategy and intent to tolerate the anxiety that comes with taking action.

"I so hate having to wait and wait in bureaucracy queues. If I refuse, I have to accept the consequences of not trying, which is no chance of getting what I want. If I wait, I can tolerate the frustration by using movement and distraction techniques. If I wait, I have a chance of getting what I want."

"Bureaucracies use ECAPs to survive. To them, I am just a number, and my relative importance is zero. If I keep my expectations realistic and expect to be treated as if I don't matter, then instinct is less likely to catastrophize. I need to anticipate that bureaucracies will always put their interests ahead of my importance."

"If I want to matter to a bureaucracy, then I need to get their attention— just enough to get them to treat me as a person rather than a number.

If I am too aggressive I will likely trigger their instinctive defensiveness. They mostly have all the power, and if it comes to a fight for survival, I will be the underdog. So, I don't have to or want to make a threat. They will use any threats as an excuse not to deliver. All I need to do to get their attention is to frustrate them."

A straightforward way to frustrate bureaucracy is to use the same excessive methods they use on you. Their primary method is the excessively complicated administrative procedures. Your method is the excessively repetitive request procedure (ERRP). You use your ERRPs to combat their ECAPs. The one who gives up first misses out. As the game plays out, you add power to your ERRP by asking for their name and employee number. Your ERRP has to generate more frustration for them than their ECAP generates for you. You need to have more room in your frustration tank than they have in theirs.

An example of an ERRP is the "broken record" technique. This method keeps repeating the same request over and over again in the fewest possible words. For example, "I want the service that you promised"; then after their lengthy ECAP explanation about why they can't provide the service, you repeat "I want the service that you promised" and so on for many more repetitions. Despite the simplicity or apparent naivety of this response, it is very powerful. This message delivers increasing amounts of frustration and pushes the listener toward their More-on Zone and into some response to avoid "losing it" in the zone. Of course, an important consideration in using an ERRP requires you to predict and keep a close eye on the receiver's level of frustration, which is potentially dangerous for your instinct.

Using an ERRP can be risky business. An excessively repetitive request procedure can get you what you want, but you had better be ready for reactions that you don't want, like outright aggression with some pushback aimed at reducing your relative importance even further. It is also quite hard to use an ERRP. It requires practice to say the same thing over and over without getting distracted, without getting drawn into your More-on Zone, without changing your words, and without saying too much each time. Your ERRP needs to be direct, boringly repetitive, and short.

"If I feel strongly enough about standing up for myself, I can prepare an ERRP and be ready to use it when they start with their ECAP excuses as to why they can't provide what they promised. But I had better make sure that my Frustration Tank level is low before I use the ERRP. I need some space between my current frustration level and my More-on Zone level to be able to sustain my ERRP. I also need to have distraction techniques to help me tolerate the pressure of my ERRP. I expect to be stressed when I use an ERRP. It is hard to do, but I am ready for it."

Action learning requires a definition of success and a way to measure progress. It encourages a focus on developing the skills needed for success, on the motivation to practice these skills, and an openness to change in the face of objective evidence.

"If I am going to risk taking action, I want to be able to determine if the risk is worthwhile. I need to define what I mean by progress and need objective ways of measuring such progress."

**Summary.**

- **Effectively dealing with bureaucracy requires you to tolerate the frustration your instinct creates in response to bureaucracies' excessively complicated administrative procedures.**
- **Move stewing thoughts into the background of your attention through a range of movement and distracting activities—doodling, reading, counting backwards.**
- **Become aware of your "shoulds" and "should nots" and question their life-and-death significance. (If you can't get the internet speed that you were promised, is that of life-and-death significance?)**
- **Use LOVE on yourself when dealing with bureaucracy (don't bother using it on it).**
- **Use ERRPs to combat ECAPs.**
- **Start the game of *Bureaucracy Snakes and Ladders*.**

## *Bureaucracy Snakes and Ladders*

If you haven't read about *Snakes and Ladders* as a game of life in Chapter 8, take a look now. It's at the end of the chapter.

# Bureaucracy Snakes and Ladders Calendar
## August

| | | 1 | 2 | 3 | 4 | 5 |
|---|---|---|---|---|---|---|
| ☐ Pure Luck<br>☐ Direct RAi<br>☐ Indirect RAi | ☐ Pure Luck<br>☐ Direct RAi<br>☐ Indirect RAi | ☐ Pure Luck<br>☐ Direct RAi<br>☐ Indirect RAi | ☐ Pure Luck<br>☐ Direct RAi<br>☐ Indirect RAi | ☐ Pure Luck<br>☐ Direct RAi<br>☐ Indirect RAi | ☐ Pure Luck<br>☐ Direct RAi<br>☐ Indirect RAi | ☐ Pure Luck<br>☐ Direct RAi<br>☐ Indirect RAi |
| 6 | 7 | 8 | 9 | 10 | 11 | 12 |
| ☐ Pure Luck<br>☐ Direct RAi<br>☐ Indirect RAi | ☐ Pure Luck<br>☐ Direct RAi<br>☐ Indirect RAi | ☐ Pure Luck<br>☐ Direct RAi<br>☐ Indirect RAi | ☐ Pure Luck<br>☐ Direct RAi<br>☐ Indirect RAi | ☐ Pure Luck<br>☐ Direct RAi<br>☐ Indirect RAi | ☐ Pure Luck<br>☐ Direct RAi<br>☐ Indirect RAi | ☐ Pure Luck<br>☐ Direct RAi<br>☐ Indirect RAi |
| 13 | 14 | 15 | 16 | 17 | 18 | 19 |
| ☐ Pure Luck<br>☐ Direct RAi<br>☐ Indirect RAi | ☐ Pure Luck<br>☐ Direct RAi<br>☐ Indirect RAi | ☐ Pure Luck<br>☐ Direct RAi<br>☐ Indirect RAi | ☐ Pure Luck<br>☐ Direct RAi<br>☐ Indirect RAi | ☐ Pure Luck<br>☐ Direct RAi<br>☐ Indirect RAi | ☐ Pure Luck<br>☐ Direct RAi<br>☐ Indirect RAi | ☐ Pure Luck<br>☐ Direct RAi<br>☐ Indirect RAi |
| 20 | 21 | 22 | 23 | 24 | 25 | 26 |
| ☐ Pure Luck<br>☐ Direct RAi<br>☐ Indirect RAi | ☐ Pure Luck<br>☐ Direct RAi<br>☐ Indirect RAi | ☐ Pure Luck<br>☐ Direct RAi<br>☐ Indirect RAi | ☐ Pure Luck<br>☐ Direct RAi<br>☐ Indirect RAi | ☐ Pure Luck<br>☐ Direct RAi<br>☐ Indirect RAi | ☐ Pure Luck<br>☐ Direct RAi<br>☐ Indirect RAi | ☐ Pure Luck<br>☐ Direct RAi<br>☐ Indirect RAi |
| 27 | 28 | 29 | 30 | 31 | | |
| ☐ Pure Luck<br>☐ Direct RAi<br>☐ Indirect RAi | ☐ Pure Luck<br>☐ Direct RAi<br>☐ Indirect RAi | ☐ Pure Luck<br>☐ Direct RAi<br>☐ Indirect RAi | ☐ Pure Luck<br>☐ Direct RAi<br>☐ Indirect RAi | ☐ Pure Luck<br>☐ Direct RAi<br>☐ Indirect RAi | ☐ Pure Luck<br>☐ Direct RAi<br>☐ Indirect RAi | ☐ Pure Luck<br>☐ Direct RAi<br>☐ Indirect RAi |

**First Move.**

You need RAi. There are three ways to get it.

- Luck—You happen to be in the right place at the right time with the right mix of attributes (looks, intelligence, vulnerability, money, availability) to collect a blast of RAi from the universe and the people in it. Your survival instinct is constantly on the lookout for these opportunities (and threats). This can happen very rarely with bureaucracies.
- Directly—you generate RAi by LOVEing yourself. You notice and make time for yourself, you accept and forgive your shortcomings, and you value yourself with something that is important to you.
- Indirectly—you generate RAi by LOVEing others. (You hope, but had better not expect that you will get some RAi in return. Demandingness is certain to dry up any source of RAi.) LOVEing others means noticing and making time for them, accepting and tolerating their shortcomings, and valuing them with something that you believe is important to them. This is most unlikely to help you when dealing with bureaucracies.

**Second Move.**

You need RAi. There are three ways to get it.

**Third Move.**

You need RAi. There are three ways to get it.

By now you can see that repetition is required to play *Bureaucracy Snakes and Ladders*. If you don't deliberately create RAi each day, you stop moving. You can only be happy if you are moving. Below you will see an example of a *Snakes and Ladders* calendar that you can use to establish a habit of generating RAi.

Each day has three boxes representing the three ways of experiencing RAi. Tick any box if it applies to your day. You only need to tick one box to enable you to move. If you have qualified to move, put a big cross (or tick) on the day.

## Landing on a Ladder.

This will happen when something *good* happens in the Luck box or in the Indirect box. You may have planned for it, but you really never know it will happen until it does. When it happens, your RAi has a burst of intensity, and you feel great. If you RAi level hits the Happiness Zone, you will be happy. You have definitely qualified to make your next move, but once again, you don't know if your happiness will last, and you don't have expectations one way or the other.

## Landing on a Snake.

This will happen when something *bad* happens in the Luck box or Indirect box. You might have worried about it happening in advance, but you never really know it will happen until it does. When it happens, you don't slide backwards in your progress; your progress just stops. Your RAi disappears, your frustration rises, and you feel bad. If you feel bad enough, your frustration may hit the More-on Zone and create collateral damage to yourself or others that further undermines your RAi.

Until you can restore your RAi, you are stuck. You are not qualified to make a move. This is the time to put your attention on your Direct box and generate RAi for yourself. Remember, you do that by LOVEing yourself, by using the strategy of cPR.

Filling out your calendar each day takes your focus off being stuck and creates a habit of moving forward. If you are moving, you will be satisfied, content, and even happy (if RAi is high enough to enter your Happiness Zone). Your good feelings will last as long as you keep moving.

# Bureaucracy Snakes and Ladders Calendar

## August

| | | 1 | 2 | 3 | 4 | 5 |
|---|---|---|---|---|---|---|
| ☐ Pure Luck<br>☐ Direct RAi<br>☐ Indirect RAi | ☐ Pure Luck<br>☐ Direct RAi<br>☐ Indirect RAi | ☐ Pure Luck<br>☐ Direct RAi<br>☐ Indirect RAi | ☐ Pure Luck<br>☐ Direct RAi<br>☐ Indirect RAi | ☐ Pure Luck<br>☐ Direct RAi<br>☐ Indirect RAi | ☐ Pure Luck<br>☐ Direct RAi<br>☐ Indirect RAi | ☐ Pure Luck<br>☐ Direct RAi<br>☐ Indirect RAi |
| 6 | 7 | 8 | 9 | 10 | 11 | 12 |
| ☐ Pure Luck<br>☐ Direct RAi<br>☐ Indirect RAi | ☐ Pure Luck<br>☐ Direct RAi<br>☐ Indirect RAi | ☐ Pure Luck<br>☐ Direct RAi<br>☐ Indirect RAi | ☐ Pure Luck<br>☐ Direct RAi<br>☐ Indirect RAi | ☐ Pure Luck<br>☐ Direct RAi<br>☐ Indirect RAi | ☐ Pure Luck<br>☐ Direct RAi<br>☐ Indirect RAi | ☐ Pure Luck<br>☐ Direct RAi<br>☐ Indirect RAi |
| 13 | 14 | 15 | 16 | 17 | 18 | 19 |
| ☐ Pure Luck<br>☐ Direct RAi<br>☐ Indirect RAi | ☐ Pure Luck<br>☐ Direct RAi<br>☐ Indirect RAi | ☐ Pure Luck<br>☐ Direct RAi<br>☐ Indirect RAi | ☐ Pure Luck<br>☐ Direct RAi<br>☐ Indirect RAi | ☐ Pure Luck<br>☐ Direct RAi<br>☐ Indirect RAi | ☐ Pure Luck<br>☐ Direct RAi<br>☐ Indirect RAi | ☐ Pure Luck<br>☐ Direct RAi<br>☐ Indirect RAi |
| 20 | 21 | 22 | 23 | 24 | 25 | 26 |
| ☐ Pure Luck<br>☐ Direct RAi<br>☐ Indirect RAi | ☐ Pure Luck<br>☐ Direct RAi<br>☐ Indirect RAi | ☐ Pure Luck<br>☐ Direct RAi<br>☐ Indirect RAi | ☐ Pure Luck<br>☐ Direct RAi<br>☐ Indirect RAi | ☐ Pure Luck<br>☐ Direct RAi<br>☐ Indirect RAi | ☐ Pure Luck<br>☐ Direct RAi<br>☐ Indirect RAi | ☐ Pure Luck<br>☐ Direct RAi<br>☐ Indirect RAi |
| 27 | 28 | 29 | 30 | 31 | | |
| ☐ Pure Luck<br>☐ Direct RAi<br>☐ Indirect RAi | ☐ Pure Luck<br>☐ Direct RAi<br>☐ Indirect RAi | ☐ Pure Luck<br>☐ Direct RAi<br>☐ Indirect RAi | ☐ Pure Luck<br>☐ Direct RAi<br>☐ Indirect RAi | ☐ Pure Luck<br>☐ Direct RAi<br>☐ Indirect RAi | ☐ Pure Luck<br>☐ Direct RAi<br>☐ Indirect RAi | ☐ Pure Luck<br>☐ Direct RAi<br>☐ Indirect RAi |

# CHAPTER 12
# RETIREMENT, AGING, AND CHRONIC PAIN

Nick has worked on the tools in his plumbing business for going on fifty years. Emily told him he should give up work a couple of years ago when the pain in his back had become a constant thing for him. Then she was getting a bit sick of his frequent moodiness and increasing periods of silence. Two years on, and it is starting to create a little bit of distance between them.

As a child, Emily had learned that offering help was a way to express love. She understood why she felt hurt when Nick got grumpy when she brought up retirement, but it had to happen sooner or later, and maybe the chronic pain he suffered would be less. Those doctors don't know everything.

Nick learned from his father the hard way that you shouldn't draw attention to yourself. That is either showing off or showing a weakness. Either way, people would take advantage of that. Nick still remembers some of the times his dad laid into him when, according to Dad, Nick "big noted" himself or "cried like a girl."

Most people wouldn't know when Nick is worrying or suffering. Emily does. She first figured it out during the global financial crises when they almost lost their house, their business, everything. She has observed it over the years since. She is affected by his moods, and she wants him to sell the business and for the two of them to live a little, travel, have fun— enjoy the success they have earned. She is a little worried that Abbey is asking her to babysit too often. Of course, she loves her grandchildren.

She just doesn't want to be taken advantage of, and she really is over changing diapers.

Nick is ready to sell the business, but at the same time, he is worrying about what happens next. His daily pain seems to be grabbing more of his focus, and he probably makes more mistakes at work than any of his tradesmen or even his two apprentices. Maybe that is a bit of an exaggeration, but he has made some costly errors recently that he should never have made.

He's afraid of being seen as old. He surfs with Jake whenever Jake does get some time away from his firm, which isn't often now that Jake is one of the managing partners. He is so proud of that kid. When they do get out together, Jake is always kidding his "old man." Although Nick and Jake are really tight, Nick wonders why he feels a bit hurt every time "old man" comes up. Nick is stewing about not being able to surf as well as he did, stay out as long as he did, and not being able to teach Jake anything more about surfing.

Nick is also worrying about Emily's plan for travelling. He would like to buy a mobile home and join the Grey Nomads. He wants to see the rest of Australia. Emily has already made it clear that she wants to travel in comfort and that means hotels with stars, nothing less than four. Nick gets it, she is a girl after all, she deserves comfort, but teleporting instantly from attraction to attraction doesn't really entice him. He wants to experience the stuff along the way. Nick wonders how he and Emily would get along in a mobile home if her heart wasn't in it. He knows she would agree if he pushed it, but he doesn't feel like he should and he doesn't feel like he should have to. She should want to.

Nick also feels that selling his business is the climax of his career, and it's all downhill after that. Sure, he would have the money, but he feels he would lose his identity, his place in the community, his purpose for getting up each day—with or without the pain. Even the desire to travel around Australia makes him a nobody in a group of old people. He even wonders about the term Grey Nomads: Why grey? Why not white or blue or red or black? There is absolutely nothing special about grey— lackluster; common; almost invisible.

Nick is not at all happy about where he is in life right now. He thinks he should be happy, given all that he has accomplished and all that he has. He is wondering what is wrong with him.

A toxic workplace is one where recognition, approval, and respect are absent. Retirement from this kind of workplace can be a great start to the rest of your life, providing you have sources of recognition, approval, and relative importance in your personal life. Retirement from a workplace that has been a positive source of recognition, approval, and respect initially results in a significant loss of satisfaction and happiness. When we retire, we leave the workers and join the "non-workers." Membership and relative importance in the new non-working group is a challenge for your survival instinct.

As we grow older, an adverse change in RAi increases because of the natural decline in physical and mental abilities caused by aging. We can't help but notice the physical evidence that we are wearing out. And what makes this worse is that other people notice as well.

Ageism is defined as prejudicial attitudes toward older people, old age, and the aging process. It reveals itself as discrimination against older people through persistent stereotypes like being unable to contribute to society, having a poor memory, being slow and inactive, being unsuitable for employment, being out-of-date, and lacking knowledge of technology.

It makes sense that once you notice you are being affected by aging, your challenge with frustration and dissatisfaction will increase. It's not easy to be happy when you are losing your energy, your resilience, your zest for life, and your relative importance.

Chronic pain at varying levels of intensity is a virtual inevitability of the aging process. It also presents as a problem earlier in life as a consequence of the universe and pure bad luck. It is a potential snake in every game of life. Perhaps the level of chronic pain you suffer has brought you straight to this chapter because you are looking for anything that might help. The idea of being happy in spite of your pain seems more than a little far-fetched. But you won't find this chapter helpful if you start here. If you haven't been able to get lasting help to lower the intensity of your pain, then you can't fix it, and you can't avoid it. The only thing you have left to work with is what's between your ears. To be able to do that, you need to read Chapters 1–8 first and then come back here. Chapter 8 is on relationships. Reading this chapter is important to managing chronic pain differently, because you need to create a different relationship with yourself.

Instinct does not see chronic pain as a threat because of the pain. Remember, instinct prioritizes survival over feelings and doesn't care if you are in pain, providing it doesn't get in the way. Instinct even approves of pain—no pain, no gain. However chronic pain, pain that never stops, becomes a threat to your survival because it distracts you from noticing things around you that are potentially lethal. Chronic pain fogs up your external threat radar and increases your vulnerability. Instinct obsesses about the threat of chronic pain through comparisonitis—"Is it any better? ... It's worse than before. ... It's just the same as before."—and reacts to these comparisons with catastrophizing—"I can't stand it. ... I might as well be dead. ... I can't go on."

Pain is an attention magnet, an invisible force that dominates your attention and draws attention from others even when you try to hide it because you are sick of being treated as a weak link. It is very hard to pay attention to anything else when you are in pain, especially when it goes on and on and on. But in the problem lies the solution. Attention is the key. Weaken the magnet effect of chronic pain on your attention, and you can be happy (well, more satisfied) in spite of it.

There is a lot between your ears that you can't control, like the unconscious interference of instinct. But one thing you can control is attention. Think of attention as a spotlight. Attention allows you to experience everything it shines on. If your attention doesn't light it up, you don't know about it, and you don't experience it. If it only partly lights it up, you only partly experience it.

Understanding the magnet effect of brief pain on attention is important to reduce frustration and increase satisfaction. Instinct uses pain to grab your attention so you will fix or avoid its cause. Paying attention to pain is important for survival. But when the magnet effect occurs because of chronic pain, the ongoing attention is a threat to survival. It increases frustration and dissatisfaction because, despite your attention, you can't fix or avoid the cause of chronic pain. Paying excessive attention to chronic pain is a threat to survival, because trying to do the impossible wears you out, and makes you less attentive and less ready to deal with new potential life-and-death situations.

If you weaken the magnet effect of chronic pain on attention, you will dilute your experience of chronic pain: less attention, less light, less pain, less fatigue, more satisfaction—perhaps even enough to be happy.

**Rubber Meets the Road.**

To maintain your recognition, approval, and relative importance as you age you need to:

- Start by getting clear about the reality of what you want to achieve. Wanting to return to being young, to being able to do the things you used to do will continuously undermine your happiness, because it is not possible in this universe. Eventually, efforts to look young will frustrate you and make you unhappy. Efforts to do the things you could do when you were young or healthy will make you unhappy. Efforts to prove your value to anyone will make you unhappy. Why? Because you cannot turn back the clock on your age and your health, and your instinct won't let you forget it.
- Look for the unconscious "shoulds" and "should nots" that are creating your frustration and undermining your RAi.
- Reality test and replace these thoughts with a perspective that allows you to get what you want (less frustration) and restore your RAi (more satisfaction).

Frustration and diminished RAi only occur when things are not the way they should be. So, ask yourself:

- What are my frustrations with aging? Look for the "shoulds" or "should nots" creating your frustration when things don't happen the way they should.
- What are the "shoulds" or "should nots" that determine my recognition, approval, and importance in this stage of my life?

**As a rule, try not to "should" on yourself or anyone else. The fewer the number of "shoulds" (or "should nots") in your life, the better for you and the better for others.**

Typical frustrations of retirement include:

- Losing a daily routine, having lost a reason for living; not having enough to do; and running out of jobs around the home.
- Not knowing what to do; wanting to do too many things and not having enough time or money to do them all.
- Losing motivation and a sense of identity.
- Demanding too much time from partners; getting annoyed at partners.
- Being treated differently by friends; feeling disconnected from past work relationships.
- Feeling anxious about undertaking new activities.

Common dissatisfactions include:

- Being faced with the reality that you have little in common with your partner; they should want what you want.
- The excitement of travel falling short of your expectations and evaporating quickly on your return. You should be able to travel more; your partner should be a better traveling companion.
- Your children taking advantage of your interest and pleasure in your grandchildren with extra childminding requests. You have done your childminding in the past, and they shouldn't be putting that responsibility on you now, not at your age.
- Your reduced income forces a change in the quality of your life—that you can't pursue passions to the same extent that you could when you were working. You should have put more into your retirement fund. You should have bought that investment property twenty years ago instead of trying to build a business.
- You no longer have the influence you had when you were working. You should have built up more networks when you were working.
- Feeling that you are experiencing the prejudice of ageism. You shouldn't be treated as if you are incompetent and invisible.

Typical frustrations of aging include:

- Tiredness, lack of energy.
- Difficulty remembering things, losing words, taking longer to find the words to express yourself, taking longer to get your thoughts out.
- Feeling judged by younger people or being treated like a child by your children.
- Getting behind with technology; people being impatient with you.
- Losing your independence, losing your driver's license.

Common dissatisfactions about aging include:

- Feeling that you don't deserve the label of "aging" or thinking that you are not old or not as old as them oldies, and you shouldn't be labeled or treated that way.
- Feeling bored with aging groups and the activities of aging groups.
- Having to move if your financial circumstances require it. The pension should be more. You should have saved more. You should have financially planned better for your retirement.
- You shouldn't have to rely on your kids looking after you, and you shouldn't have to be in a position where strangers are looking after you.
- Your kids owe you; they should take care of you.

Typical frustrations of suffering chronic pain include:

- The disabling effect of pain on everything you do.
- Constant fatigue and lack of motivation, being unable to concentrate.
- Not being able to sleep.
- Forgetfulness.
- Making mistakes because of the distraction of pain and stewing about it.

Common dissatisfactions about chronic pain include:

- Loss of a job, mobility, patience, status, credibility (unlike a broken limb, chronic pain can't be seen).
- Loss of relationships, security, and faith.
- Grieving for all the losses caused by the chronic pain.
- Being unable to stop stewing about the unfairness and injustice of it all.
- Feeling weak, anxious, angry, or depressed.
- Seeing oneself and one's life as being permanently affected.

**Psychological Resuscitation**

**Step 1 of cPR: Calming Frustration.**

While the perspective and restoration required to resuscitate happiness will be different from situation to situation, achieving small *c*, a little bit of calm, is the first and necessary step regardless of the situation. Movement and distraction are great activities for attaining small *c*; see Chapter 7 for details on getting small *c* and to remind yourself of the risks of drug use.

**Step 2 of cPR: Perspective on RAi.**

A look at the three dimensions of RAi will help Nick better understand his distressing perspective of retirement and aging. He asks these questions of himself.

The first question is about being noticed:

- *Am I sensitive about recognition in retirement?*

"Who am I when I retire? Another grumpy old man? Another RV Retiree, Snowbird or Grey Nomad?"

The second question is about approval:

- *Am I sensitive about loss of approval when I retire?*

"Will people think that I am just not up to it anymore?"

The third question is about importance:

- *Am I sensitive about my importance after retirement?*

"Builders come to me when they have a problem. Is that going to stop when I retire?"

"My influence on others will stop the moment I give up my business. How am I going to feel about that?"

"I have always been the provider in my family. I won't be any longer. How will that reality affect me?"

You have to first bring these thoughts to the surface before you can moderate the collateral damage that they cause.

**"To learn the secrets of life, we must first become aware of them." (Albert Einstein)**

Below are examples of surfaced thoughts that, once identified, can be normalized to moderate instinct's sensitivity to retirement and aging.

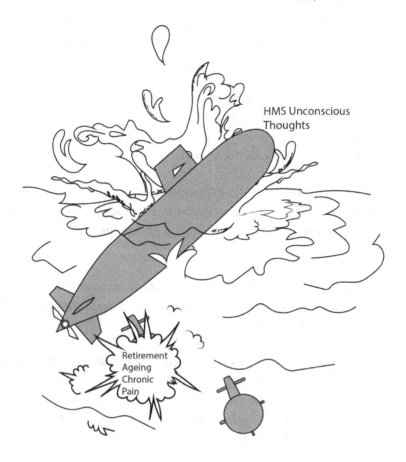

You may identify with some of them. You don't need to find all of your instinct's comparisonitis and catastrophizing. All you need to do is to identify a small number of clear thoughts that highlight instinct's fear. The work we do with a few will generalize to all of them and prepare us to move on to restoration.

Examples:

"I understand that instinct sees routine as necessary for achievement and essential for relative importance. It notices when my activity slows down and catastrophizes that I am in danger of losing approval and support."

"Instinct doesn't know how to rate my relative importance now that I have retired. It has noticed people treating me a little differently and is catastrophizing about what this means."

"There is a real difference in my life now that I have retired, and it is healthy and necessary for instinct to be worrying about losing relative importance and with it security. Under these circumstances, I should be feeling insecure and anxious about making new connections."

"Instinct expected that traveling together would create a better bond with my partner and increase my relative importance in my relationship, but all we do is fight. When we do share a good time, the good feeling never lasts."

"My kids are only using me as a babysitter for my grandchildren. Instinct thinks that I shouldn't be taken for granted and that my retirement should be for me, not for my kids."

"I should have more money to do the things that I want to do. Instinct is so critical of me for not being good enough to provide a better life in retirement. It's so unfair; life was so unkind to me. And I am so pathetic for ruining the opportunities that I had. I made the wrong choices, and I should have done it differently."

"Instinct interprets my lack of influence in retirement and lack of 'buying' power to pursue my interests as evidence of a loss in relative importance. This is confirmed by the changes in the way I see people treating me. It is understandable that it is catastrophizing about this, and that I am feeling frustrated and dissatisfied."

"On occasions when I might feel confident about the future, I won't be surprised if instinct spoils it. Getting approval is not enough for instinct. I should expect that any satisfaction that I get from making an effort to enjoy my age will start to deteriorate when instinct winds me up again and causes me to be dissatisfied with my relative importance. Instinct doesn't allow for rest. Being safe is not enough; it wants me to stay safe."

"If I accept the necessity of sometimes feeling bad about aging, I can stop trying to avoid these feelings, accept them, and focus more on thinking about what I can do the next time I feel bad and what the outcomes are that I want."

### Step 3 of cPR: Restoration of RAi

Perspective on missing RAi will normalize your instinct's catastrophizing and prepare you for the goal of restoration. Restoration of satisfaction and happiness when faced with retirement, aging, and chronic pain requires you to:

- Restore recognition.
- Restore approval.
- Restore importance.

Restoration requires:

- An openness for action.
- A willingness to take risks.
- A determination to learn from outcomes.
- An ability to improvise and adapt.

Dealing with unwanted circumstances can lead to such intense levels of frustration that you readily get to the point of giving up. If you get stopped by your bad feelings, you can get moving again by following the restoration routine of risk-taking and action learning.

Effective risk-taking requires you to:

- Assess the possible consequences of your actions before you take them.
- Put a value on the worthiness of the risk.
- Work up the courage to take the risk.
- Have in place strategies to tolerate the anxiety associated with the proposed risk.

A method of measuring the value of a risk is to estimate the balance between the anxiety of taking the risk (the downside) and the future satisfaction from taking the risk (the upside). If you are likely to be satisfied with the future consequences of your action, and you can tolerate the frustration, it's worth taking. If you are likely to be dissatisfied with future consequences, then it's not worth taking. Even if you are satisfied now, you need to think about future satisfaction. Satisfaction today is not worth dissatisfaction tomorrow.

You don't require a crystal ball to evaluate risks. All you need do is take some time and think about possible future consequences. Action learning requires a definition of success and a means of objective measurement of progress. It requires a focus on acquiring the skills needed for development, the motivation to practice these skills, and the openness to keep adapting efforts in the face of objective evidence.

The restoration ideas and strategies that you plan and put into action only need a possibility of success. You are not going to come up with a plan that guarantees minimum frustration, satisfaction, confidence, and happiness, because 84,000 things in your environment will continue to affect the outcome. This means that no matter how carefully you plan for an outcome, something may still go wrong.

**LOVE is the default restoration strategy.**

The acronym of LOVE will move you through a course of action that will restore your RAi in retirement and through the process of aging.

**L**—stands for listening in an active way. Active listening requires you to surface your instinctive concerns and reflect on what you are thinking.

**O**—stands for overlooking. Reducing the disapproval that you have for yourself and for others when your interests clash will moderate the catastrophizing impact of instinct. To do this, you need to consciously remind yourself that things are mostly not life-and-death. This reality test helps you tolerate instinct's conclusion that your concerns about the impact of retirement and aging are really not that important; you have been aging since birth.

**V**—stands for valuing. When decide that your concerns are normal and natural and not indicative of your weakness as a human being, you significantly restore your RAi.

**E**—stands for effort, consistency of effort. Instinct will continue with comparisonitis and even accelerate it during aging. Expect to have moments of intense concern, and keep reminding yourself of the naturalness of these moments. Make time for regular self-LOVEing.

Like it or not, routine provides a daily schedule and purpose and optimizes opportunities to maintain your relative importance. If you are good with routines, it will be straightforward enough to create a weekly routine that keeps you busy in retirement. If you had hoped that one of the good things about retirement would entail being free of routine, then creating one for yourself and sticking to it is going to take more effort and initially more frustration.

The following thoughts are examples of restoration ideas. For them to be useful, action has to follow.

"I understand that instinct sees routine as necessary for achievement and essential for relative importance. It notices when my activity slows down and catastrophizes that I am in danger of losing approval and support. I can calm instinct by creating and sticking to a simple routine. I expect it to be frustrating at first, but if it comforts instinct and increases my motivation and energy levels, it is worth it. I can tolerate the initial frustration of taking action by using exercise and distraction strategies."

"This routine is my choice. It's not being forced on me, and I can stick to it or not stick to it. If I don't feel like it, I won't do it. But I realize that if I stick to it most of the time, I will feel better about myself. A routine gives me something to look forward to, or not look forward to, but either way, I will feel prepared to make the most of my retirement."

"Instinct is noticing my increased criticism and dissatisfaction with my partner since I have been home more. It is catastrophizing that we have nothing in common, nothing to talk about, and that life from here on will only get worse and will become increasingly unbearable. It is telling me that I can't stand it. No wonder I am feeling unhappy and, yes, I can do something about that. I can find new interests and new activities with my partner and with others. I will not expect my partner to be the only source of relative importance in my life."

"My kids are only using me as a babysitter for my grandchildren. Instinct thinks that I shouldn't be taken for granted and that my retirement should be for me, not for my kids. I can remind instinct that although being taken for granted lowers relative importance, providing a valuable service increases relative importance. I enjoy spending time with my grandkids."

"I should have more money to do the things that I want to do. Instinct is so critical of me for not being good enough to provide a better life in retirement. It's so unfair. Life was so unkind to me, and I am so pathetic for ruining the opportunities that I had. I made the wrong choices. I should have done it differently. Shoulda woulda coulda—it is what it is! I don't have to catastrophize about past decisions. The fact that I am alive today means that they weren't life-and-death situations. Whenever I find myself thinking about them, I will use exercise and distraction to push them into the back of my mind. I don't want to stop instinct—I can't—but I will put its concerns in the back row of my attention. My retirement is a time for me to live differently today, and I am not going to use it to dwell on yesterday. I know how to reduce the frequency of my stewing." (See Chapter 7.)

"I can avoid my son getting upset with me if I just agree with what he wants for me. But if avoiding it today makes it worse tomorrow, it is not worth it. I can tolerate my son's frustration, and if I stick to what I want, I will be satisfied tomorrow. I have to keep repeating myself over and over until it gets through to my son, and if I count backwards when he is talking, I can lessen the effect of his frustration on me."

"When other people stereotype me because of my age, I can use the stereotype to get what I want. If I want a seat, I can use my age to influence people into giving me one. If I want to be noticed, I can fake being distressed. If I want more time to think or more help, I can feign not understanding and request further explanation. Instinct doesn't want anyone to think that I am needy, not coping, or not understanding, and so my acting this way will stress my instinct out a little. If I am ready for the anxiety I feel when drawing attention to myself, I will be prepared to release the intensity of my feelings with movement and distraction."

**Summary.**

**Being contented, satisfied, and happy in retirement, and with or without chronic pain in your later years requires:**

- **Realizing that your instinctive concerns about the loss of RAi are normal, and everyone has them.**
- **An ability to release spikes of frustration with techniques to achieve little *c*.**
- **Developing routines to maintain cPR in the background and knowing how to use cPR as a reaction to difficult moments that will come your way.**
- **An ability not to take the behavior of others toward you personally. They are affected by their instinctive fear just as you are ("Someday I will be like that" or "There but for the grace of God go I.")**
- **Beginning *Hokey Pokey Snakes and Ladders*.**

### *Hokey Pokey Snakes and Ladders*

If you haven't read about *Snakes and Ladders* as a game of life in Chapter 8, take a look now. It's at the end of the chapter.

# Hokey PokeySnakes and Ladders Calendar

## August

| | | 1 | 2 | 3 | 4 | 5 |
|---|---|---|---|---|---|---|
| ☐ Pure Luck<br>☐ Direct RAi<br>☐ Indirect RAi | ☐ Pure Luck<br>☐ Direct RAi<br>☐ Indirect RAi | ☐ Pure Luck<br>☐ Direct RAi<br>☑ Indirect RAi | ☐ Pure Luck<br>☐ Direct RAi<br>☑ Indirect RAi | ☐ Pure Luck<br>☐ Direct RAi<br>☑ Indirect RAi | ☐ Pure Luck<br>☐ Direct RAi<br>☑ Indirect RAi | ☐ Pure Luck<br>☐ Direct RAi<br>☑ Indirect RAi |
| **6** | **7** | **8** | **9** | **10** | **11** | **12** |
| ☐ Pure Luck<br>☐ Direct RAi<br>☑ Indirect RAi | ☐ Pure Luck<br>☐ Direct RAi<br>☑ Indirect RAi | ☐ Pure Luck<br>☐ Direct RAi<br>☑ Indirect RAi | ☐ Pure Luck<br>☐ Direct RAi<br>☐ Indirect RAi | ☐ Pure Luck<br>☐ Direct RAi<br>☐ Indirect RAi | ☐ Pure Luck<br>☐ Direct RAi<br>☑ Indirect RAi | ☐ Pure Luck<br>☐ Direct RAi<br>☑ Indirect RAi |
| **13** | **14** | **15** | **16** | **17** | **18** | **19** |
| ☐ Pure Luck<br>☐ Direct RAi<br>☑ Indirect RAi | ☐ Pure Luck<br>☐ Direct RAi<br>☐ Indirect RAi | ☐ Pure Luck<br>☐ Direct RAi<br>☐ Indirect RAi | ☐ Pure Luck<br>☐ Direct RAi<br>☐ Indirect RAi | ☐ Pure Luck<br>☐ Direct RAi<br>☐ Indirect RAi | ☐ Pure Luck<br>☐ Direct RAi<br>☐ Indirect RAi | ☐ Pure Luck<br>☐ Direct RAi<br>☐ Indirect RAi |
| **20** | **21** | **22** | **23** | **24** | **25** | **26** |
| ☐ Pure Luck<br>☐ Direct RAi<br>☐ Indirect RAi | ☐ Pure Luck<br>☐ Direct RAi<br>☐ Indirect RAi | ☐ Pure Luck<br>☐ Direct RAi<br>☐ Indirect RAi | ☐ Pure Luck<br>☐ Direct RAi<br>☐ Indirect RAi | ☐ Pure Luck<br>☐ Direct RAi<br>☐ Indirect RAi | ☐ Pure Luck<br>☐ Direct RAi<br>☐ Indirect RAi | ☐ Pure Luck<br>☐ Direct RAi<br>☐ Indirect RAi |
| **27** | **28** | **29** | **30** | **31** | | |
| ☐ Pure Luck<br>☐ Direct RAi<br>☐ Indirect RAi | ☐ Pure Luck<br>☐ Direct RAi<br>☐ Indirect RAi | ☐ Pure Luck<br>☐ Direct RAi<br>☐ Indirect RAi | ☐ Pure Luck<br>☐ Direct RAi<br>☐ Indirect RAi | ☐ Pure Luck<br>☐ Direct RAi<br>☐ Indirect RAi | ☐ Pure Luck<br>☐ Direct RAi<br>☐ Indirect RAi | ☐ Pure Luck<br>☐ Direct RAi<br>☐ Indirect RAi |

Hokey Pokey
Snakes and Ladders
Calendar

**First Move.**

You need RAi. There are three ways to get it.

- Luck—You happen to be in the right place at the right time with the right mix of attributes (looks, intelligence, vulnerability, money, availability) to collect a blast of RAi from the universe and the people in it. Your survival instinct is constantly on the lookout for these opportunities (and threats).
- Indirectly—You generate RAi by LOVEing others. (You hope, but had better not expect, that you will get some RAi in return. Demandingness is certain to dry up any source of RAi.) LOVEing others means noticing and making time for them, accepting and tolerating their shortcomings, and valuing them with something that you believe is important to them.
- Directly—You generate RAi by LOVEing yourself. You notice and make time for yourself, you accept and forgive your shortcomings, and you value yourself with something that is important to you.

**Second Move.**

You need RAi. There are three ways to get it.

**Third Move.**

You need RAi. There are three ways to get it.

By now you can see that repetition is required to play *Hokey Pokey Snakes and Ladders*. If you don't deliberately create RAi each day, you stop moving. You can only be happy if you are moving. Below you will see an example of a *Hokey Pokey Snakes and Ladders* calendar that you can use to establish a habit of generating RAi.

Each day has three boxes representing the three ways of experiencing RAi. Tick any box if it applies to your day. You only need to tick one box to enable you to move. If you have qualified to move, put a big cross (or tick) on the day.

**Landing on a Ladder.**

This will happen when something *good* happens in the Luck box or in the Indirect box. You may have planned for it, but you really never know it will happen until it does. When it happens, your RAi has a burst of intensity, and you feel great. If you RAi level hits the Happiness Zone, you will be happy. You have definitely qualified to make your next move, but once again, you don't know if your happiness will last, and you don't have expectations one way or the other.

**Landing on a Snake.**

This will happen when something *bad* happens in the Luck box or Indirect box. You might have worried about it happening in advance, but you never really know it will happen until it does. When it happens, you don't slide backwards in your progress; your progress just stops. Your RAi disappears, your frustration rises, and you feel bad. If you feel bad enough, your frustration may hit the More-on Zone and create collateral damage to yourself or others that further undermines your RAi.

Until you can restore your RAi, you are stuck. You are not qualified to make a move. This is the time to put your attention on your Direct box and generate RAi for yourself. Remember, you do that by LOVEing yourself, by using the strategy of cPR.

Filling out your calendar each day takes your focus off being stuck and creates a habit of moving forward. If you are moving, you will be satisfied, content, and even happy (if RAi is high enough to enter your Happiness Zone). Your good feelings will last as long as you keep moving.

# Hokey Pokey Snakes and Ladders Calendar

## August

| | | 1 | 2 | 3 | 4 | 5 |
|---|---|---|---|---|---|---|
| ☐ Pure Luck<br>☐ Direct RAi<br>☐ Indirect RAi | ☐ Pure Luck<br>☐ Direct RAi<br>☐ Indirect RAi | ☐ Pure Luck<br>☐ Direct RAi<br>☐ Indirect RAi | ☐ Pure Luck<br>☐ Direct RAi<br>☐ Indirect RAi | ☐ Pure Luck<br>☐ Direct RAi<br>☐ Indirect RAi | ☐ Pure Luck<br>☐ Direct RAi<br>☐ Indirect RAi | ☐ Pure Luck<br>☐ Direct RAi<br>☐ Indirect RAi |
| 6 | 7 | 8 | 9 | 10 | 11 | 12 |
| ☐ Pure Luck<br>☐ Direct RAi<br>☐ Indirect RAi | ☐ Pure Luck<br>☐ Direct RAi<br>☐ Indirect RAi | ☐ Pure Luck<br>☐ Direct RAi<br>☐ Indirect RAi | ☐ Pure Luck<br>☐ Direct RAi<br>☐ Indirect RAi | ☐ Pure Luck<br>☐ Direct RAi<br>☐ Indirect RAi | ☐ Pure Luck<br>☐ Direct RAi<br>☐ Indirect RAi | ☐ Pure Luck<br>☐ Direct RAi<br>☐ Indirect RAi |
| 13 | 14 | 15 | 16 | 17 | 18 | 19 |
| ☐ Pure Luck<br>☐ Direct RAi<br>☐ Indirect RAi | ☐ Pure Luck<br>☐ Direct RAi<br>☐ Indirect RAi | ☐ Pure Luck<br>☐ Direct RAi<br>☐ Indirect RAi | ☐ Pure Luck<br>☐ Direct RAi<br>☐ Indirect RAi | ☐ Pure Luck<br>☐ Direct RAi<br>☐ Indirect RAi | ☐ Pure Luck<br>☐ Direct RAi<br>☐ Indirect RAi | ☐ Pure Luck<br>☐ Direct RAi<br>☐ Indirect RAi |
| 20 | 21 | 22 | 23 | 24 | 25 | 26 |
| ☐ Pure Luck<br>☐ Direct RAi<br>☐ Indirect RAi | ☐ Pure Luck<br>☐ Direct RAi<br>☐ Indirect RAi | ☐ Pure Luck<br>☐ Direct RAi<br>☐ Indirect RAi | ☐ Pure Luck<br>☐ Direct RAi<br>☐ Indirect RAi | ☐ Pure Luck<br>☐ Direct RAi<br>☐ Indirect RAi | ☐ Pure Luck<br>☐ Direct RAi<br>☐ Indirect RAi | ☐ Pure Luck<br>☐ Direct RAi<br>☐ Indirect RAi |
| 27 | 28 | 29 | 30 | 31 | | |
| ☐ Pure Luck<br>☐ Direct RAi<br>☐ Indirect RAi | ☐ Pure Luck<br>☐ Direct RAi<br>☐ Indirect RAi | ☐ Pure Luck<br>☐ Direct RAi<br>☐ Indirect RAi | ☐ Pure Luck<br>☐ Direct RAi<br>☐ Indirect RAi | ☐ Pure Luck<br>☐ Direct RAi<br>☐ Indirect RAi | ☐ Pure Luck<br>☐ Direct RAi<br>☐ Indirect RAi | ☐ Pure Luck<br>☐ Direct RAi<br>☐ Indirect RAi |

Hokey Pokey
Snakes and Ladders
Calendar

# CHAPTER 13
# THE HOLY GRAIL

One of the things that prompted me to write this book is the daily frustration I have with myself about my moods. I discovered my interest in psychology around the age of 16 when I had a compulsory meeting with a school guidance counselor to discuss further study and future life. The academic requirements of high school were a no-brainer for me. I was an unmotivated student, because my interests were primarily surfing, football, athletics, and girls. So, I relied on a good memory and three nights a week of homework to get by. My marks were just above average, and I had no intentions of going on to college.

While I was waiting to see the guidance officer, I picked up a book on psychology that was on his coffee table. Wow. I was so absorbed by that book and must have said so, because he lent it to me for a few weeks. Psychology didn't seem to have much in common with surfing, football, athletics, and girls, and I have wondered many times since then what attracted me so much to that book. I have concluded that my conscious mind and my instinctive, unconscious mind were already looking for ways to get on better together. For example, I knew then that I should be working harder at school, but I didn't. I knew my school results were significant for my future, but I just couldn't control the urge to have fun, and studying was not fun.

Despite my piqued interest in the psychology book, I dropped out of school. A couple of years later, I went back to night school, and a couple of years after that, I managed to gain entrance into a university. Three degrees and nine years after that, I was a qualified and registered clinical psychologist with fair amount of life experience—relationships and children—under my belt. Over the years, I have received positive feedback from my clients and my students. Apparently, I am a good therapist and lecturer. So, with all this knowledge of psychology and experience as a therapist, how come I have made all the mistakes that my clients and people in general make, and why haven't I been happy?

I have concluded that I am just like everyone else, protecting myself from perceived inadequacies by busily sticking my head in the sand and being driven by the same unconscious survival needs. Knowledge, wisdom, experience, success, and accomplishment are all things occurring at a conscious level. The instinctive need for recognition, approval, and relative importance occurs at a subconscious level. There is an overlap, but it's limited. You can't change the automatic reactions of your unconscious, but you can regulate them.

There is no Holy Grail for happiness, because instinct sees happiness as a threat to survival. Happiness equals contentment and if we snooze, we lose … our life. Yes, that's a bit extreme if we are not living in life-and-death situations, and most of us aren't. But that's how our instinct has evolved over thousands of years, and it is what it is.

So, if we are not living in a life-and-death situation, how do we moderate the unconscious interference of instinct on the quality of our life? What we cannot do is change or prevent it without seriously awful side effects. Drugging will nullify instinct, but mostly that just gets us killed eventually. What we can do is get real with our expectations and manage the interference of instinct that has to happen with cPR.

Realistic expectations need to be based on the acceptance of comparisonitis and catastrophizing occurring continuously without our awareness; on the necessity of distress to power our reflexes; and on the fact that instinct prioritizes survival over happiness. Accepting this leads to the following expectations:

- You should be frustrated and dissatisfied daily. Without these feelings, you are not adequately prepared for the next threat to come along.
- When you are satisfied and feeling happy, instinct will undermine these feelings through comparisonitis and catastrophizing.
- You can moderate the impact of comparisonitis and catastrophizing with cPR and extend periods of satisfaction and happiness.
- You can expect to feel satisfied and happy, but no matter what you do, you cannot expect it to be continuous.
- When contentment and happiness naturally begin to fade, trying to control the universe in order to sustain them will make you more discontented and unhappy.
- If you stop fretting about fading satisfaction and happiness, you will be more open to the next opportunity to experience them.

You can't hear your unconscious, but it can hear you.

If you consciously strive to accept the occasions of feeling bad as necessary and healthy for survival, then you can reach the point where frustration, anxiety, anger, dissatisfaction, and low mood become ho-hum moments in your life. Once you stop stewing about feeling bad, its duration lessens and frees up your attention to appreciate new possibilities of recognition, approval, and relative importance. You are more likely to feel good more often, but remember: Don't expect it to last.

Regulate the impact of your instinct by lowering the emotional intensity of its interference and use perspective to tag its causal influence on your current feelings and state of mind. Stop blaming others and circumstances for how you feel. Use restoration for the intent and the action necessary to generate the recognition, approval, and relative importance required to calm and reassure your instinct. This process will always be necessary. No matter how many times you have already done it, you will need to do it again. There is no off switch for instinct. It has evolved to keep you alive, and it will do its job as best as it can regardless of how you feel.

Nevertheless, you can be happy in spite of it.

Printed in the United States
By Bookmasters